THE HEART

The Final Destination

JULIE ANDERSON

ICAN Publishing Company
San Diego, CA

The Heart: The Final Destination
Copyright ©2007 Julie Anderson

All rights reserved. No part of this publication may be reproduced, transmitted, transcribed, stored in a retrieval system, or translated into any language, in any form, by any means, without the written permission of the author.

Preface Copyright ©2007 Peter H. Karlen

Cover Art and Cover Design by Julien Wells

Published by
ICAN Publishing Company
7520 Charmant Dr.   Suite 1014
San Diego, CA 92122
858-658-0446

Library of Congress Control Number: 2006938925

ISBN # 0-9792090-051995

Praise for "The Heart"

Julie's book describes new ways to understand and practice unconditional love without which we have nothing. She gives easy-to-understand examples of how we can improve our lives and practice this love on a daily basis. I highly recommend that everyone read and follow the techniques in this book.
Dr. Edward F. Group III, DC, ND, DACBN
Founder and Med. Dir. of Global Healing Center

This precious book of wisdom illuminates one's path to live and love from the heart. It is a poignant reminder that in every moment we need to return to our hearts in how we think, speak, and act. I have found an indescribable joy and peace in applying the principles of this book to my daily life.
Adele Honchor
Real Estate Investor

Do you remember those magical moments when you had the clarity and courage to follow your heart's desire - no matter what? Wouldn't it be nice if you had a special friend who stood beside you and reminded you of those times, believed in you completely, and in whose presence you felt stronger, more capable, and alive? Julie Anderson is that friend who teaches us how to be our own best friend. She reminds us of our greatness, and, by sharing inspirational personal experiences and practical exercises, provides the map that leads us back to the heart, our final destination.
Sheela Hewitt
Founder & Director, Fallsburg Wellness Center

Simply reading Julie's book opened my heart, reminding me of a gentle loving way to be with myself and with the world. For those who strive to live from their heart, this is a must read.
MaryAnn Kilmartin, MSW
Dir. Electromagnetic Biofeedback Inst.

Acknowledgements

This book is dedicated to Gurumayi Chidvilasananda, the spiritual head of Siddha Yoga. It is Gurumayi who has been my inspiration and who continually lights my way and guides my spirit on the path of love.

I am deeply grateful to all the unseen great beings who ever so gently and lovingly inspired me to put on paper the words of my heart.

From alpha to omega I had the encouragement, wisdom and support of Ruth Mullineaux, Sheela Hewitt, Melodie Hurlen, Adelle Honcher, Judy Duthie, Loretta Lanphier, and Stefen Nastarowicz and last but not least my precious family. To these wonderful friends I offer my love and special thanks for helping me complete one of my heart's desires.

A special thanks to Peter H. Karlen, my greatest cheerleader in creating this book. His unerring wisdom, clear direction, confidence in me and gentle yet often humorous encouragement kept me pursuing the dream of offering this work. In the preface Peter wrote for this book he brings together the golden threads of all religious traditions and spiritual paths. This heartfelt being, a La Jolla attorney of integrity and with a spiritual understanding so rooted in consciousness, was a divine intervention for this book being published. He has patiently listened to my ideas, challenges, and joys of putting this book together. Without Peter entering my life, this book would not be in your hands today.

My gratitude and appreciation go to Julien Wells, my beautiful son-in-law for the exquisite cover artwork. I feel this cover will stir the soul that is seeking inner, world peace and universal peace. Stepping into our heart and starting to love from within will transform the world without.

Then there are myriads of special individuals who have touched my life and have been the best well-wishers anyone could ask for along with all who participated in the events and experiences to make this book possible, I thank you all.

Foreword

When all is said and done, the only thing that truly matters is what is in your heart. Everything you say, think and do, up to the point where you are ready to transition out of this world, is recorded there and radiates from your being like a beacon.

Living from your heart is a new way to think, and feel, and act. It is in fact the whole point of life. This is such an essential truth that it would seem no more needs to be said. And yet, contemporary life pulls us from our heart center on a daily basis. We become overloaded with responsibilities, frustrated by lack of time, debilitated by personal disappointments, and hardened by what seems like an uncaring world. But if we wish to experience life to its fullest, we need to step into the heart and live from the standpoint of love for everyone and everything upon this plane of existence. The heart is our final destination, and this book is a guide on how to stay on its divine path, even as we are pulled to stray.

For me, this book is a demonstration of coming from my heart and listening to my inner wisdom, even as I struggled to make sense of the impulse. About a year ago, while sitting by myself in front of a fire in a Catskill Mountain log home, the title of this book flashed through my mind like lightning. The vision shocked me. I had no intention of writing a book. Still, I took this message as a hint that I should start writing, **NOW**. I struggled and struggled and got nowhere fast. After weeks of trying, I put the pages I had written on the shelf and forgot about them.

The next spring, I moved to California after living in a monastary for five years. I was diligently concentrating on starting my healing practice when, during my meditations, I began receiving information to put everything aside and write. I was leery to say the least. I felt I needed to establish my practice, and my previous attempt at writing this book proved fruitless. But I acceded to my inner wisdom and sat down at my computer that day. For the next 6 weeks, I worked 8 to 10 hours everyday, almost 7 days a week.

When I felt I had written all I was capable of doing, I lovingly tied a beautiful satin ribbon around the manuscript, laid it on my altar, and offered it to God. I wondered why I was able to write this book then and not months or even years earlier? After contemplating, I realized I needed to step more into that place of pure love which I was going to write about and to "walk my talk" even more fully. I am not perfect; I still make many mistakes. But the point is to try – every single minute of every single day – to align myself with the highest intentions, thoughts, and acts.

Living from the heart is a conscious decision and takes practice. But it is not a task; it is a joy. There is no better state of existence on this planet. This book lays before you the divine possibilities of transforming an ordinary life into an extraordinary one. I offer you blessings and love on your journey into the heart – your final destination.

Preface

For almost four hundred years a maxim of Western philosophy has been "cognito, ergo sum," meaning "I think, therefore I am." This idea, which equates being with thinking, has profoundly affected how people conceive of themselves and their world.

Under this conception every child is taught, almost from birth, how to think and behave and to identify with her thoughts. The young child learns good and evil and to judge others. With language, the child's inchoate world is artificially categorized, analyzed, and divided. Though the child could perhaps see the world "face to face," soon the magic disappears and the veil is irrevocably cast over her eyes. Like Adam and Eve, for a small morsel of knowledge the child is expelled from enchantment.

Yet, despite years of training on how to think, discriminate, and behave, few have ever been taught to feel or act from the heart rather than from the head. At school hardly anyone is taught the heart's wisdom, and even religious practices rarely cultivate it, though sermons and scripture tell us to love our neighbors, avoid judging others, and renounce worldly attachments. Seldom can those who listen live by this wisdom no matter how often repeated. Perhaps the reason is we learned it by rote, not by feeling, in contrast to spiritual beings like Christ and Buddha for whom this wisdom was innate and heartfelt. But here is a book from which heart-based living can be experientially learned, step by step.

Julie Anderson's book is about living from the heart in everyday life. Each of the 27 chapters is devoted to a special aspect of "heart-based" living. Incidents abound from the author's life and other lives which illustrate the themes, and each chapter ends with exercises which readers can use to experience a "heart-based" existence in their own lives. The great variety of incidents and experiences will make most readers aware of how their every thought, word, and deed echoes throughout the world and how much life is made up of moral choices, moment by moment. These recounted everyday experiences also show that inner and outer peace have the same source, living from the heart.

Though the book draws upon a variety of religious and spiritual traditions, perhaps the purpose of this book is best reflected by St. Paul when he rhapsodizes in praise of love.

"When I was a child, I spoke as a child, I understood as a child, I thought as a child: but when I became a man, I put away childish things.

For now we see through a glass, darkly; but then face to face: now I know in part; but then shall I know even as also I am known. And now abideth faith, hope, and love, these three; but the greatest of these is love."
(I Corinthians ch. 13)[1]

As St. Paul knew, any chance of living in the spirit of heartfelt charity, compassion, and love is often extinguished early in life when truth is hidden behind a veil and one can only see through a glass darkly. Perhaps that dark glass is the illusion of knowledge, particularly the notion that most problems can be solved by thinking them through rather than accepting a heart-inspired solution. As this book shows, the problems everyone faces, ordinary or extraordinary, are often solved through a leap of faith, whether doing a good deed without recognition or reward or surrendering one's possessions or even one's life to God.

Eighteenth century philosopher Immanuel Kant proclaimed that our knowledge of the world is woefully incomplete and will always remain so because it is derived from our five limited senses of sight, hearing, touch, smell, and taste. Yet, other senses exist, often possessed by animals, including the ability of some to sense magnetic fields or to return to faraway nesting grounds, and many animals experience entirely different realities though extraordinary senses of sight, hearing, and smell. Though complete knowledge of the world will always escape us, profound emotional wisdom can be attained. The path of the heart has already been trodden by the great prophets, and its milestones are non-attachment, forgiveness, non-judgment, gratitude, humility, and compassion. As this book demonstrates, even the most impossible conditions can be overcome by applying the wisdom of the heart. This wisdom is dramatically illustrated by the story of a woman about to lose her house to a terrible storm; instead of panicking, she blesses the house and thanks God for all her wonderful years at home and then peacefully departs with only a few meager possessions.

The holy books of various religions have praised God for infinite wisdom but also for mercy and compassion. In comparison to God's infinite knowledge, no man or woman, nor mankind as a whole, can ever achieve even the smallest measure. But even the humblest of souls can possibly achieve divine emotional qualities and the actions which flow from those qualities, i.e., love and compassion and their gift of forgiveness and mercy.

Until wisdom of the heart is not only known but also felt, peace will not flourish, for the heart of change is the change of heart. Neither science nor technology threaten our existence but lack of emotional wisdom. Though feeling this wisdom comes as grace for the few, it eludes the many no matter how hard they try. This book, therefore, seeks to provide inspiration and guidance to those who seek emotional knowledge. It does so by offering real life accounts of courage, forgiveness, compassion, and humility, perhaps best exemplified by Joan, a victim of the worst concentration camps who experiences forgiveness and beauty in the midst of unimaginable squalor and horror.

This work stems not so much from scholarship as from experience. Though the author has spent years following her teachers' spiritual guidance and could have merely restated their teachings, her writing comes from intense experience and reflects ideas and practices she applies to her own life. Through her awareness Ms. Anderson is able to follow the heart's path whether at work in a retail store, in the privacy of her own home, on line at a restaurant, or in a taxi on the streets of Bombay. The beauty of this book is in showing how important it is to act from the heart even in one's daily routine and in the "smallest" of life's incidents. Throughout, the book demonstrates that wisdom of the heart is nurtured in the routine incidents of life, when one remembers to be grateful for the gift of a pinch of salt or remembers to bless every living creature in sight including the leaves of a distant tree. For life is not so much the grand traumas and triumphs but rather the moment-to-moment existence defined by one's feelings and state of being.

Though this book provides the theory and practice of heartfelt living, one of its lessons is that acting from the heart is not just a conscious behavioral choice but reflects a state of being. That is, the doing flows from the being. Yet that state of being is often only achieved from doing those things which mirror the heart, then experiencing the results. As this book shows, when actions come from the heart, they reflect its perfection. As St. Paul wrote at the beginning of his chapter on love:

"Though I speak with the tongues of men and of angels and have not love, I am become as sounding brass, or a tinkling cymbal... Love never faileth; but whether there be prophecies, they shall fail; whether there be tongues, they shall cease; whether there be knowledge, it shall vanish away. For we know in part, and we prophesy in part. But when that which is perfect is come, then which is in part shall be done away."

This book promises neither success, health, or prosperity; rather it offers a journey to harmony and Self-discovery. By gradually absorbing the wisdom of the heart and its use in everyday life, and by carefully practicing the exercises, life is transformed. Sometimes transformation may come even after mastering a single exercise, perhaps one involving gratitude or meditation, or even patience. After all, a person living from the heart in pure humility, practicing non-judgment of others, or trusting God's will can achieve that singleness of vision referred to in scripture. As Lao Tzu said, "There are many paths to enlightenment. Be sure to take the one with a heart."

Yet even for those who seek worldly gain, there is treasure here. As explored by many writers from Dale Carnegie[2] to Daniel Goleman,[3] emotional intelligence leads to success more often than academic prowess. But emotional intelligence is not merely praise, flowers, cards or gifts but heartfelt kindness without hope of return. It is a state of being where every action emanates from genuine regard for others, so the person acting from the heart is friend to both the humble and the exalted. For that person realizes at some deep level that although there is self and other, at the same time there is no other but Self.

A great philosopher once analogized a human life to a wave breaking on the shore, striking the shore with such promising force and reaching up to the land with tentacles of water, only to pitifully recede. For each of us the challenge is to learn the knowledge of the heart early, long before the wave retreats into the sea from which it came. By reading this book, learning its truths, and practicing its lessons you are now on that path to enlightenment, the one with a heart.

Peter H. Karlen, La Jolla, California, February 2002

[1] "Love" has been substituted for "charity" in this King James translation, as Prime Minister Tony Blair did in his reading at Princess Diana's memorial service.
[2] "How to Win Friends and Influence People."
[3] "Emotional IQ."

TABLE OF CONTENTS

1. Does Your Heart Welcome Each Person with Love? **3**
2. Does Your Heart Live in Courage? **9**
3. Does Your Heart Live in Faith? **17**
4. Does Your Heart Listen to Others? **23**
5. Does Your Heart Live in Beauty? **31**
6. Does Your Heart Live in Compassion? **37**
7. Does Your Heart Live in Humility? **43**
8. Does Your Heart Live in Wisdom? **47**
9. Does Your Heart Live in Patience? **53**
10. Does Your Heart Live in Gentleness? **59**
11. Does Your Heart Live in Gratitude? **67**
12. Does Your Heart Live in Enthusiasm? **75**
13. Does Your Heart Give Blessings? **81**
14. Does Your Heart Take Care of Others? **87**
15. Does Your Heart Forgive Others? **93**
16. Does Your Heart Love the Animals? **101**
17. Do You Let Your Heart Smile? **107**
18. Do You Follow Your Heart? **113**
19. Do You Let Your Heart Meditate? **121**
20. Do You Live From Your Heart? **127**
21. Do You Speak From Your Heart? **131**
22. Do You Love Your Heart? **137**
23. Do You Think With Your Heart? **143**
24. Do You Act From Your Heart? **149**
25. Do You Work From Your Heart? **155**
26. The Physical Heart **161**
27. The Walls of the Heart **167**

Just BE from the Heart **173**

About the Author **175**

Index **179**

CHAPTER 1

Does Your Heart Welcome Each Person With Love?

This is one of the greatest teachings of all time. I love this practice. With <u>everyone</u> I meet during the day, when our eyes first meet, I mentally say to them, "I love you with all my heart." This is such an exhilarating experience. Then no matter what happens I have anchored myself in the space of my heart, whether it be an uplifting exchange of love or information or a challenge; like being put in a position of having to reprimand a child, or telling someone something they may not want to hear.

The interesting aspect of this whole process is that very seldom do I run across people who do not reciprocate this welcoming space of love. I do know that like attracts like, and since I am putting out love as much as I possibly can, I feel it comes back to me a thousand fold. The people I attract in my life are of like mind. Of course, every once in awhile I meet hurtful, complaining, and unhappy folks, but I know I am there to add a bit of love in their life and to be that example of "Yes, you are loved no matter what space you are in."

It's a lot easier to welcome someone with love if they are welcoming us with the same love, but what happens when they don't? Those are the times when you just open your heart and arms; knowing that the other person is giving the only thing he can in that moment. Welcome him, offer what you can, and then move on. Nothing was lost for you and everything was gained. You stayed in your heart, you got to feel good about trying to make his day a little brighter, and you gave the other person a wonderful opportunity to receive love. Whether he accepted or rejected that love was up to him.

I want to let you in on a secret of mine that makes so many people shift their attitude around me when I meet them. I swear to you it works every time. Trust me and try it.

I'll bet this scenario has happened to you a hundred times. You get in line at a fast food chain, get up to the counter and are asked, "How can I help you?" with about as much enthusiasm as a wet rag. You simply give them your order, pay, step aside, and wait for your food while the counter clerk hollers in a drone, "next?" Over the years I've noticed that customer service is getting better in some ways. Oftentimes now when you approach a counter person they will have a smile on their face and greet you with what I call "pasted-on" enthusiasm. In other words, if they do not smile and act really glad to see you they will lose their job. At least this is a step in the right direction because if you are taught to smile at and act enthusiastic with each and every customer or else, it does become a habit and a good one, which over time starts to carry over into your personal life. You find you are naturally beginning to smile more, and when you smile more you become happier.

Now lets change the above scene. I will give you an example of what happened to me just the other day, but let me give you my secrets first.

1. *Genuinely smile* at the other person and mentally send love.

2. *Use their name, look into their eyes (this is very important), and greet them.*
"Hi Tom, how are you today?"
Then wait for a response (which can be positive or negative). You would be surprised at what they tell you even if the line is a block long. Here you are in front of them and you actually care about what they are feeling! This can be a shock to them because they usually feel they don't even count in the big scheme of things.

3. *Say something uplifting or encouraging to them.* Relate to them wherever they are mentally, such as: "You're really doing a great job handling all these people so efficiently" or "It must be really difficult to deal with all these people with such a bad headache." You will be surprised at the results this brings.

Let me set the stage for something that happened recently. Fast food vendor, long line, and only one person working the counter. I have an agenda to meet but I am trying to wait patiently knowing she is doing her best. I get to the counter and this girl looks at me as if she would just as soon throttle me or anyone else standing in front of her.

"Hi Louise, this looks like a pretty stressful job. How do you hold it together?" She stopped, startled for a split second, and then said, "Yes, you're right. I am totally stressed out. People are so rude and impatient, and I'm the only one here. Two staff called in sick today, and I've been standing here for the last five hours without a break." I replied, "I understand what that is like; I did this type of work myself when I was young. It can take a lot out of you. Be sure to be really good to yourself today when you get off work. You deserve a treat." She got this huge smile on her face and said, "Thank you. Where are you from?" After I told her, she said, "I knew you weren't from around here. People aren't that nice here." And then with an upbeat expression she asked, "What can I get for you?" She not only gave me what I asked for but a ton of extra french fries. It was her way of showing appreciation for my honoring and acknowledging her.

Don't we all like to be given good strokes? We love the compassion that others offer us. In that space we unite, we become as one.

Think of a time when someone just looked into your eyes and said, "Welcome, I'm glad you're here." In India the word "namaste" is used in greeting someone. This is a simple word but complex and beautiful in its meaning. Often when "namaste" is used they touch their hand to their heart at the same time. This one word means, 'I honor the God in you and know you honor the God in me. When we stand in that space of love together you and I are one.' How profound. This is actually what we are saying to one another when we look directly into someone's eyes and say "Hello and welcome." Do it with meaning and the true feeling that there is no one on this earth at that minute who you would rather be with.

If your life is not based on this simple practice, you are missing the whole point of existence on earth. To welcome each person with love is such a sublime way of honoring every individual we connect with, whether it's for two seconds or two hours, and can set the stage for the rest of your conversation. It is the highest offering you can make to another individual in any moment.

Inspiration Exercises:

♥ Take a moment and close your eyes. Now imagine each one of the people you will encounter today, each family member, each friend, all work mates individually, even those with whom you have differences, and then mentally stand in front of each one and say, "I love you with all my heart." Thoughts know no time or space. When you say that to them mentally, they receive your thoughts in their energy field and actually receive your love.

♥ On seven post-it notes write: "I love you with all my heart." Place these in strategic places like on the kitchen microwave, bathroom mirror, bedroom, nightstand, car dash, and desk at work. Use your imagination. This will get you in the habit of remembering to say this phrase mentally all the time to everyone you meet. Each time you see a note put a picture of someone different in your mind's eye. Even if you don't feel this love from your heart for everyone, keep practicing. In time it will become a beautiful habit and eventually will come from your heart.

♥ Today, every time you are waited on or are serving others, use the person's name and greet them as you look into their eyes. Ask them how they are today and then respond in a very loving and gentle way, or just say "I understand."

♥ Take time this evening to reflect on the effect any of the above exercises had in your encounters with others. How did you feel about yourself when you were able to greet others with love? Everyday try to increase the number of times you remember to mentally say, "I love you with all my heart," to everyone, even strangers you encounter. Do not be hard on yourself when you forget. It will soon become a habit and will have an effect on every exchange you make. (Remember that your pets and animals also appreciate your loving them with all your heart, too.)

CHAPTER 2

Does Your Heart Live in Courage?

To have a courageous heart takes both great gentleness and great strength. Our life is about change. Life is continual unending change. Yesterday was different from today and today will be different from tomorrow. Nothing in this world is static. People are born. People transition out. You had a job yesterday. You lose it today. You feel great today. Tomorrow you are diagnosed with cancer. You had a gorgeous home yesterday. A hurricane destroyed it today. On and on it goes, the cycle of change. How do we cope? How do we go on? What allows us to continue with life in the midst of heartbreak and crisis?

I'm going to enter the realm of courage through the avenue of change. How many of us like change? For most of us we would just like things to stay status quo for a little while, especially in this day and age where it seems we never have enough time. Even establishing a routine can be a challenge. We rush from here to there and back again. Time has speeded up and we are trying to go faster and faster to keep up with it all. This world is changing so fast and now more than ever before we are seeing the effects of change all around us, all the time, from continual tremendous natural disasters to terrifying upheavals in our own back yard.

Most people fear and resist change. As events continue to happen and shape our lives we begin to feel like we have no control and we begin to live in fear, but change is good for us. It helps us grow and transform our lives for the better, which is what life is all about. Change is about stepping out of fear and stepping into courage - the courage to grow.

When confronted with change we often think we are alone, feeling helpless and lacking the knowledge of how to accept and deal with circumstances that are often beyond our control. Here is where the courageous heart comes into play. It takes a courageous heart to know that you aren't alone. Surrender is the key that unlocks the courage of the heart to go forward. When you resist life, you are saying no to the flow of life. Surrender and start saying Yes! Let go and make room for transformation and magic to unfold. Ask God, your guides, and angels for the courage to learn what it is you need to learn from each situation, and to accept any change as an opportunity for growth.

This reminds me of one of many huge changes in my life that I wasn't prepared for, a divorce from my husband. I chose, however, to believe and surrender to the fact that this would be for the better and would allow each of us to grow, which it did. But the change that came after that was the one I want to share with you.

After the divorce I was bound and determined to keep this huge house that we both had purchased. This was my dream home, the home I wanted to raise my children in and to live in for the next thirty to forty years - even if I had to do it by myself. Not only was I going to keep it up but continue to remodel it, keep the yard groomed, raise my two small children, and work full time. Piece of cake! Not quite. I am a determined person, but this turned out to be a little too much for my feeling that I could be superwoman. I was becoming more exhausted with each passing day. I prayed to God for help because I could not see a solution to my dilemma, as I wanted to stay in this house. Then one day, several weeks later, someone at work asked me how I was doing with adjusting to the divorce and taking care of the house and all. I stated, "Oh, I'm going to sell the house." I sat there totally stunned at what I had just said. Where did that come from? There was no way on earth I was going to sell that house. However, I was so puzzled by my own statement that I really began to contemplate it.

I knew there was a reason the universe had said those words through me. I also know that when one door closes another one opens. I slowly started to embrace the concept that maybe a change would be good for me, so I made a conscious decision that there would be another home that I would love even more than this one. I sat down and listed what I wanted as a single parent: more time with my children, no more yard work, close to work, good schools, excellent child care, etc. I began to visualize our new life and I surrendered my newfound ideas to God and asked for this or something even better to materialize. The minute I surrendered, miracles began to happen. My house sold immediately and we ended up in a beautiful new condominium that I loved. The grounds were beautiful, the schools were excellent and I now had time to play and be with my children - more time in fact than when I had been married and had someone with whom to share the chores.

Now mind you, never in a million years would I have even thought to live in a condominium. I was too rooted to living on that perfect corner lot in a two-story doll house home, with its white fence and window planters and shutters on every window. To entertain the idea of condominium life was absurd. But you know what? It was one of the best things I ever did. I can look back now and see what an albatross that house was in preventing me and my children from living a happy and productive life. When I embraced change with a courageous heart I was supported in ways I had never dreamed possible.

Another aspect of courage I would like to address is that of standing in your truth. When something isn't right, or you see a situation that is hurtful, or that you could alter, do something about it. Now I'm not talking about putting your own life in danger but there are many instances that each one of us have simply ignored because we did not want to become involved, or we lacked the courage to say something that may have backfired on us.

Let me give you an example of how I now approach these situations. I was sitting in a local pizza parlor in a fairly rough neighborhood and several tables away a father was sitting with three young children. He persisted on being extremely abusive to the children, yelling and screaming at them, telling them how bad and awful they were. I could hardly stand it. I wanted to take each of those kids and hug them, and tell them how special they were. Well as fate would have it, all of a sudden the littlest one, a girl about five years of age came over to me and stood by my table. I patted her head and said, "I just want you to know how wonderful I think you are." Just as I said this the father yelled at her, "Who are you bothering now? Get back over here." As I passed their table on my way out, the father commented, "How would you like to have these rotten kids?" I stopped, turned around and looked directly at him and his children, and from the courage and gentleness of my heart I stated, " I would absolutely love to have your children. They are beautiful beings and should be treated as such." There was absolute silence. The kids looked at each other and then began to snicker. Their dad just sat there stunned. I turned around and walked away.

In my younger days if someone had asked me that question I probably would have just laughed as I continued to walk by, or I would have sympathized and said something like, "It looks like you have your hands full," and exited quickly. We must begin to take the courage of our heart and stand up for what we believe is right. Every time we let an opportunity pass us by where we do not come to the aide of others we have also hurt ourselves. We need to step out of fear and into truth.

We must learn to live in the courage of our heart in many ways, from speaking up in setting the truth straight, to calling on the strength of the heart for the courage to go on in the face of all obstacles. Through this courage we can accept the changes in our life with the understanding it is for our own soul's growth. This courage of the heart helps us to live in peace and know that all is well.

Inspiration Exercises:

- ♥ Sit quietly and think of three major, challenging changes that have occurred in your life. Write them down. Now ask yourself how you made it through those changes and write your answers. You obviously made it through them or you would not be here reading this exercise. What was it exactly that helped you get through the rough times? Friends, faith in God, your own perseverance of just getting through each day, or even each hour. Somewhere in the midst of it all you stepped out of your fear, anger, frustration, sadness, jealously, or whatever feeling comes up for you and into the courage to keep going, the courage to surrender, the courage to be content with what you have and not what you do not have.

  Now take that situation and reflect on how it allowed you to grow. Write out your answers. After a period of time, sometimes it may take a year or two, you'll see that if that particular change had not happened, you would not have grown. This is sometimes very difficult to see but in every single situation you can carry it to the highest and see the outcome as a beautiful-sometimes difficult-heartfelt growth experience. You'll see how your courage to get through took place, either subtly or not so subtly. Let that be your guide for other changes coming into your life.

- ♥ Write down a challenging situation you are presently going through. Next, jot down ways of looking at it from a positive standpoint. An example may be that things are all of a sudden not going right at work... perhaps the universe wants you to make a change and get a better job. Or perhaps your lover has decided to fall in love with another... look at it as a gift and how you may benefit from this experience. Undoubtedly down the road you will be grateful it happened when it did. Time will show you reasons for these events and how these changes resulted in your growth. Someone may be waiting for you who is even more special than you ever dreamed possible. Surrender your challenge to God, the angels, your guides and ask them for the lesson and for help to get through your situation. The help will always, always, always be there.

❤ Write out three different instances where you failed to show courage, in which you could have said something that would have stated your truth in a very compassionate and straightforward way that would have helped others, yet you chose to remain silent, ignore the situation, or just walk away.

Perhaps someone was inappropriate to another and you remained **silent**. Maybe a child was being yelled at or abused and you just shook your head in disbelief that others could treat a child like that, and then you went on your merry way.

Perhaps you did not aid someone in a situation that was detrimental to him or her such as watching that person being bullied and you just stood there observing, or **walked away**.

Maybe an inappropriate comment was made that hurt another's feelings and you just **ignored** the situation, sided with the person whose feelings were hurt, and said nothing to the offender.

Now for each one of those instances write out how you could have approached it differently, standing in truth, helping to make a difference in another's life - helping others to learn they cannot get away with inappropriate behavior.

As you practice this type of behavior you will begin to feel more comfortable and gain more ideas on how to speak up effectively. This does not mean yelling at someone or talking vindictively to another, but genuinely stating the facts of the truth as it comes from your heart. You may still witness situations where you do not speak up, but with the practice of taking any inappropriate situation and dealing with it from a higher space you will feel more at ease with speaking up and helping to make this world a better place to live.

CHAPTER 3

Does Your Heart Live in Faith?

Faith is an inner knowledge that is found deep within your own being. It inspires and uplifts you in all circumstances of life. Faith is a dynamic energy that magnetically attracts spirit to create a union with the Divine.

This unseen force that has such incredible power is one of the most mystical and mysterious of virtues. It is an acceptance or conviction of a teaching as a true belief. You cannot hold it in your hand and say, "Let me check this one out." It comes from an understanding that there is a divine power that perfectly runs this universe and knowing that you too hold a very valuable place in its existence.

On the other side of faith is doubt. Doubt can be viewed as a destructive power when it keeps you in poverty, fear, worthlessness and limitation, or even more destructive when it turns you against God. After reviewing these last two sentences perhaps I should rephrase them. Some people have faith in poverty, thinking they have to struggle throughout this life. Many, many beings have faith in fear: fear of life, fear of change, fear of being hurt, fear of failing, fear of humiliation, and the big fear of who or what they truly would be if they could only step out of fear. Some individuals have the faith that they are unworthy and go through this life playing a victim of their own beliefs.

What about the doubt that keeps you away from your divine birthright of becoming one with God? So many people live in anger against that which they feel to be an unjust and unloving God, who they feel has created such anguish and strife in this world. When we are born on this earth plane a veil descends over us. We forget who we truly are and for what purpose we came here. We feel stranded and left so alone. The root cause of all our pain is this separation from God. When our questioning and our longing become so intense as to our purpose for being here and we begin to ask for God's guidance, we find the veil of ignorance being lifted and begin to find ourselves once again being connected to our source. Every single person upon this earth has a divine plan of his own, and to be able to connect to it requires faith. When you turn your doubt about God's purpose around and ask for help instead of throwing your anger at God, miracles begin to happen. Problems and irritations will always continue to exist on the physical plane but you will begin to see them from a different perspective. You will be able to meet your challenges with a new and higher awareness and attitude that was not available before. Faith attracts faith. Call upon God for faith. Prayer alone will create faith - faith in yourself, faith to step out of limitation and fear and into the love in your heart.

Don't go down the road of doubt, doom and gloom. Look at doubt as your enemy, a dark force that creeps into your consciousness to separate you from your faith. Have this absolute faith that your life is being guided by an unseen force that is so powerful that when it is directed in the highest way all things are possible for you.

A quick story on faith. It was only my second trip into the city of Bombay from the ashram where I lived. I needed to go in for some work I was doing. At 6:30 a.m. I got on our van with two other people who were Indian and knew their way around the city. Directions are not a strong suit of mine and I asked one of my fellow travelers for directions for one of the errands I needed to run. Now, if any of you have ever been to a city of this magnitude in a third world country you can understand how challenging it might be to give someone directions. They go something like this: Go to a street called… then go behind such and such a shop and then behind that shop is another shop and behind that is an alley that leads to a compound that leads to a building that has a sign that says… go past that sign and up some rickety steps behind the family's kitchen and… Do you get the drift? Bombay is built in layers upon layers.

Anyway, we arrived in Bombay two-and-a-half-hours later and we went our separate ways. The main mode of transportation in this city is by taxi and I continued to get to all the places of business I needed to go that day until I only had the one place left I had asked directions to that morning. One learns quickly to always ask the taxi driver if, number one, they speak English and number two, do they really know where such and such place is. I did this and got a nod and mumbling of yes, yes, yes. You can guess the rest. The driver could speak no English except for the word yes and I quickly began to realize he didn't know a thing about where I wanted to go. Before I knew it we were totally lost. He just kept driving and trying to ask other drivers at my insistence through hand motions. I was now in a section of this city that I knew nothing about and Bombay goes on forever. I became dehydrated and absolutely exhausted from being in 120 degree heat all day, in and out of taxis with no air conditioning, inhaling smog (the 2nd highest polluted city in the world). I bowed my head and said, "God, I need some help here. I'm lost. I'm tired. I have only one hour to get this errand done and to find the van to go home which will leave at 4 p.m. whether I am there or not. I have no idea where I am and the driver as you know, does not speak English. What do you want me to do? I totally surrender to your will. Thank you."

As I was praying we were slowly creeping through streets where literally thousands of people were walking everywhere. You couldn't tell where the sidewalks were or if there were any. I told the driver to stop (one of the few words I know in Hindi). He did. I then made an instant decision that this was not where I wanted to get out. There were just too many people and the energy was just too chaotic. I told him, "Drive on", giving him a hand gesture to go forward. He did. In a few minutes we were finally driving along an area that had huge tall cement walls lining both sides of the street and there were only hundreds instead of thousands walking around. I told the driver to stop again. He did. I closed my eyes for a split second to try to gather my thoughts and all of a sudden I heard this voice say to me, "Julie, What are you doing here? You are in the middle of nowhere and you almost drove over my feet." I opened my eyes and there, leaning in my window was one of the Indian boys I had come in with. In a city of over 13 million people I stopped right in front of one of the two people I knew in this city. Now what are the chances of that happening? He hopped in the taxi, took me to where I needed to go, and then we proceeded to the van for our long trip home. Thank you God.

This was one of the greatest lessons in my life to have absolute faith that I am being watched over, cared for, and that God does hear every sincere prayer and that I am not the one in charge here.

Faith is the unseen force that guides you and works in a realm that is beyond human understanding and reason. I can only tell you from my own experiences that if you pray for faith to bring you faith it will happen. This one act of praying to have faith is a magnet so powerful that it will immediately attract spirit, making possible a union between you and God.

Inspiration Exercises:

- ♥ Put yourself in my situation in India of being sent into this huge city to do several projects by your employer. Just try to imagine what it would feel like in 120 degree heat, your clothes wet from sweat and sticking to you, you are lost, exhausted, hungry, and no one who could speak your language to understand or direct you to an English speaking area - no one even knows what language you are speaking! What would you have done? Would you have cursed the elements or your employer for putting you in this predicament, or would you have kept persevering even though you were in a space of sheer exhaustion? Or would you have had the courage to absolutely surrender and thank God for this test of faith and ask for guidance? We all have situations in our lives that we can relate to in an instance like this. Reflect on a personal situation that overwhelmed you. What did you do? If you did not ask for divine guidance, can you imagine what would have happened if you had?

- ♥ Bring a situation to the forefront of your memory in which you feel absolutely helpless, or a situation that is irritating you, or one in which you feel a change has to be made in your life regarding a circumstance. Take this situation and look at all the aspects of it, how you got there, what are your options as you see them, how you could help yourself, then talk them over mentally or out loud to your guides, angels, Jesus, Allah, Buddha or whomever you feel an affinity to. Then surrender to faith that you will be given the answers. The answers are there.

As you practice faith and surrender to this great divine power, you will begin to have more faith that your life is divinely guided. You are never given more than you can handle; and often times as you begin to rely on this faith, your life becomes so much easier that you begin to understand you are not alone. Once you understand you are not alone there will be such an amazing peace that dwells within you that nothing can disturb it.

♥ Every morning surrender your day to God and ask for faith to be firmly established in your life, to know that all is of the divine plan. Then three times during each day surrender any challenge that comes along, whether big or small, to this divine power. Ask for guidance, give thanks that it is forthcoming, and release it. Before you retire to bed this evening review what you surrendered during the course of the day. How did the events turn out? If you do not have a challenge resolved before going to sleep, ask for divine guidance for the highest outcome before falling asleep. Do the same thing tomorrow and the next day and the next. This will begin to transform your life.

CHAPTER 4

Does Your Heart Listen to Others?

Every human being alive wants to be listened to, but how many of us really feel heard when we do speak? Listening to others from your heart is a habit that can be learned. When you do come across someone who puts their entire focus on you and truly listens to you as if you were the only person in the world, isn't it like the feeling of being loved? You feel like, "Yes, someone is actually listening to me; someone finally understands what I'm trying to convey." It feels good to be heard. Blessed are the people who know how to listen.

Each individual is a reflection of universal life force, and each person's deepest yearning is to be loved and valued. For this to happen we need to be heard. So when you truly listen to another you are honoring that individual and her deepest yearnings to be heard. You are showing her compassion in a positive way by saying to her, "You are important to me and I am willing to hear what you feel, think, and believe." When people feel heard, they feel good and they feel cared for. Simple listening skills can create a world filled with harmony.

This is what therapists are trained to do. They listen to your challenges, not necessarily to solve them but to genuinely listen to them. Often times just through someone who listens and asks a few questions back to you, you yourself can solve your own challenges. In actuality it is all listening and rephrasing.

I am going to give you some tips on how to be an effective listener, and how to give feedback to build better communications. Effective listening skills should be taught in every grade school, junior high and high school around the world.

To be a good listener you first have to stop talking yourself. Most people are so concerned about talking about themselves that it is often hard to get a word in edgewise. It is a far wiser move and a much richer experience to let others talk. Give your tongue a break and begin to listen for a change.

When you do have a conversation with someone:

Face them directly.
Gaze into their eyes with rapt attention.
Listen to what they have to say with all your heart.
Rephrase what they say to make sure you understand them correctly (So often we misinterpret what another is trying to convey to us.)
Don't sound like a parrot repeating what they said, but read between the lines and offer back what you felt they were trying to say.
Don't interrupt them with a thought of yours or an analogy that you may feel is relevant. Just listen with no agenda of your own.
Don't finish sentences or words for them.
When they are finished, pause, gather your thoughts, and then you can begin to speak.

If you can learn these simple rules of listening, you will be miles ahead of the rest of the world. When you need to give feedback to someone, this is the greatest way I have found to do it in a non-evasive way. Think of a situation where you want to convey something to someone. Take a moment and become consciously aware of what your emotional reaction is and then begin.

1. I feel… Describe how you are feeling about the other person's behavior. Always use "I" because it is <u>your</u> feeling. These feelings are usually described as anger, hurt, fear, confusion, joy and so on.

2. When you… Describe the actions or behavior and why you think it matters. Simply state the facts without judgment and how this affects you or your work.

3. Would it be possible… Propose a possible solution or action the other person could consider. (Would you be willing to… or, Perhaps you might…)

4. What do you think? Listen to what the other person has to offer. Don't judge their responses, but come to a mutual agreement on the future desirable action. If a person needs time to think about it, get back to them.

Here is an example. *I feel* overwhelmed and frustrated *when you* approach me with problems the minute I walk into the office in the morning *because* I have not even had a chance to take my coat off and get settled. It would be so helpful to me *if you could* just welcome me in the morning and give me five minutes to get settled at my desk before telling me what I need to address that day. *What do you think?*

Next step: How does one become open to receiving this type of communication?

1. Acknowledge what was said. Let the other person know you understood what was said. "I hear that it stresses you out when I bombard you with problems the first thing in the morning."

2. Acknowledge the points that were made. "You are right, I do start telling you about all of the challenges of the day before you get settled."

3. Think about the situation or respond with an agreed upon course of action. An example might be, "I'll think about my actions and see if I can come up with an idea on what may work for both of us" or, "I understand how that must feel to you, and yes, I can wait until you are settled at your desk for the day before I tell you what has happened."

Remember that good listening skills are an art. It is an art that needs to be cultivated and practiced. Have fun with this. Get a friend to practice with you. I have known couples and families that by practicing these communication skills have dramatically improved their personal relationships. You are actually stating and owning your feelings, beliefs and thoughts without imposing, or accusing, or forcing others to accept how you feel they should be or act. When you can communicate or offer feedback to someone in this style, you will have the opportunity to hear and to be heard.

When I was working in retail, I can remember many instances when customers would come in and be furious over something. No matter where I was, the team would somehow find me to deal with these difficult customers. I loved the challenge.

There was never a time that I could not get someone to calm down, and they would inevitably walk away with their anger dissipated. The way I did this is that I would look directly in their eyes and say, "I can tell you are really upset. How can I help you?" (And I meant it). I would rephrase their frustration, show compassion, and usually within a minute they were at a space where they could listen and we could communicate equally with one another. At that point I could begin to help resolve the problem.

Too often people approach a problem or situation with the expectation that no one is going to listen to them. In such circumstances people are quite agitated and are determined that their case will be heard or else there will be hell to pay. We can't fight fire with fire. We must learn to listen to others no matter how ridiculous the situation may appear. Often times people don't care if you give them something in return, they just want to be heard.

Blessed are the beings that are good listeners. Find someone to practice with and have fun with it. Learn to be a good listener. Everyone will love you for it.

Inspiration Exercises

- ♥ Four times today consciously take the time to simply listen to someone with no agenda of your own. This may prove quite difficult for most people. Just listen and only listen. See how the other person reacts. This can be done without the other person even knowing what you are doing. It will give you an opportunity to see how often you feel like interrupting, or want to finish off a word or sentence for them.

- ♥ Tomorrow at least four times, listen to another with no agenda of your own, truly listening, but then rephrase what they said. Remember not to parrot what someone has said or they will catch that you are up to something and usually resist sharing any further. An example you could use that works well is, "So, what you're are telling me is…" This can often be astonishing. We so often interpret something totally different from what was intended by the one speaking. Rephrasing what they just said clarifies that you heard the message correctly. This can be done without anyone understanding what you are trying to accomplish or learn.

    Keep practicing each one of these traits until you become an expert at them - listening and rephrasing.

- ♥ Using the guidelines given for feedback, practice with a friend or family member very deliberately. If both of you can come to an agreement to give feedback to one another in a loving and compassionate manner, you will end up in a beautiful long-term cherished relationship. Remember that in any relationship you can always lovingly agree to disagree with one another.

♥ Take several instances that have recently happened to you in which you would like to have given feedback and didn't. Write them down and using the four steps, write out your feedback approach. Now pretend you are giving feedback to that person. Then take it one step further and approach the individual in person. Often times it can still be appropriate even if a week or month has gone by. The more you practice this the more comfortable it will become and you will eventually be able to do it automatically instead of having to consciously think about it.

CHAPTER 5

Does Your Heart Live in Beauty?

The world is full of beauty when the heart is full of love. Doesn't everything in life feel beautiful if you are happy and content? Yet you can be in the most challenging circumstances and still experience the beauty of the heart. You could live in a cement block and see its beauty. It's all a matter of choice. One person looks at a rose and sees it as a miracle. Another person sees thorns and thinks God made a mistake. It's how you respond to circumstances that count.

I know of no greater example of seeing the beauty in the most severe of circumstances than the story of a woman I met about 10 years ago. I will call her Joan. I was staying at her home, a bed and breakfast, when I noticed a set of numbers tattooed on her arm. I asked her about them, knowing full well what they were. She proceeded to tell me of being a teenager in the concentration camps in Germany. It was a tale so tragic and cruel you could only wonder how she survived.

At the age of sixteen, right before her eyes, her family was captured, separated, taken away and eventually killed. Being young and healthy, she was shipped off to work in the concentration camps under subhuman conditions. There, as the captives became weak and ill, the number tattooed on their arm was called and their clothes taken away. They were herded naked into trucks, often times in subzero temperatures, and taken to Auschwitz, where they met their death.

Joan remembers that when this happened, most everyone knew where they were going. Although extremely scared, most were ready to die. They were sick, worn down, and stripped of every shred of human decency. She, though, through an absolute miracle and will to live, escaped by jumping out of one of these trucks and sliding down an icy ravine.

She was later recaptured and this time forced to work underground for eighteen-hours a day in an industrial complex. When someone became too weak to work, they were thrown into the wide-open cesspool that everyone used as a toilet, and left to die. They lived as slaves, men and women crammed into one large open room. No bathrooms, except for the cesspool. No showers. Lice and open sores often covered their bodies. The stench and fear they lived in was immense.

Through all of this, Joan continually tried to remember tiny bits of beauty in her life. Sometimes, after being underground for weeks, she would have an opportunity to get just a glimpse of the sky. The beauty of that one sight would so fill her with joy that she would live on that image for days.

She also tried to uplift those around her. Instead of seeing the filthy matted hair and open sores, she would look at the beauty in their hearts. There was no clean water with which to wash, but she would reach down into a puddle of muddy water, dip her finger in it and dab it on her face. This dirty water did nothing to actually clean her face, but the act itself, the intention behind it, to honor herself and God, made her feel special.

For me, Joan's story represents the beauty of the heart to overcome any hardship. She obviously survived the holocaust, and when I met her she was filled with the joy of life. She was married to a wonderful man and lived in a lovely home, which she offered to share with others.

Joan took her experience of pain and torture, incorporated into her heart these difficult lessons, and moved on with her life. She spoke at high schools and events around the world, sharing her story in a loving and compassionate way in the hope that people would not forget what can happen if they do not take care of one another. She taught that no matter how bad their life might be at any given moment, there are others who are still less fortunate. She implored people to count their blessings, to see beauty in even the smallest of things because sometimes it may be all you have to hang on to. She taught that all things change, so not to be discouraged in adverse conditions.

I truly admired this woman because she personally remembered some of the people who had tortured her and knew they were alive and well and living anonymously in high governmental positions in Germany. She was aware that some of the families of these men had no idea what they had done to torture others. But she felt it was not her place to judge them. She has never revealed any of their names for fear of hurting and disgracing their families. She forgave all who had been cruel to her and wished them well.

The beauty of the heart is never marred no matter what occurs. Your outer circumstances may be so challenging you may not want to go on with life. But if you can just drop into your heart and know there is a higher purpose for all things that happen, you can choose to see the beauty even amidst the darkest night of the soul. All things shall pass. Things will change in this world; sometimes for good and sometimes for what does not feel for the good. But you can always look for the beauty whether it be in the lesson you are learning or from something physical in your midst. If you can do this, your awareness of the preciousness of all of life will be vastly enhanced.

Take a minute and think of all the beauty that surrounds you. Now absorb that in your heart. It is yours forever.

Inspiration Exercises

- ♥ Take a moment to shut your eyes and begin to mentally scan all the beauty that exists just within the room you are in. Really think about this. For example: Even if you are in some dull governmental office is there a glass on the desk? Think of the gift that alone is. Something we can hold in our hand and drink out of. Then think of the beauty of your hand that can hold a glass, that you have a hand to hold it with.

- ♥ Do this exercise for all the beauty you can potentially see in the space you are in, even to seeing the beauty in the light bulb overhead. It gives you light - to see your children or friend, to read by, to be able to do your work or hobby by. You will soon realize that doing this exercise in any room in your home could easily occupy most of the day. Let this awareness of beauty fill you with gratitude.

- ♥ Other beings living outside of Earth's realm refer to it as the "Blue Planet", and a very sought after place to experience. It is my understanding from reading many books that it is the most beautiful planet in this galaxy, and when you consider that there is estimated life on over 10 million planets in this galaxy alone, one begins to develop a much broader awareness of its immensity and beauty. Go outside and just sit on the grass or the beach and drink in the beauty of the grains of sand, dried seaweed, trees in the distance, flowers, chipmunks and grasshoppers. Keep developing your sense of beauty in all things. It will keep your heart singing.

- ♥ Take a situation that is affecting you deeply at present or one from the recent past, and instead of rewinding and playing it again and again, over and over, in you mind shift your awareness a bit to stepping into thinking about something positive. Start looking at the beauty of what surrounds you and dwell on these things instead. Maybe it's something as simple as the pattern on your wallpaper that is beautiful to you, or the cover on a CD you enjoy, or your fun vehicle. How did it get there? How was it designed? Take items back to their origin and think about how many people it took to get it in front of you. Start thanking each and every one for their part in making your world more beautiful. The more you begin to shift your awareness to something uplifting, the more you'll be filled with gratitude; and the less you will be giving energy to negativity around any situation, making your own life more beautiful.

CHAPTER 6

Does Your Heart Live in Compassion?

Compassion is one of the most exquisite words in the human language. To have it and display it is one of the greatest virtues a human being can offer to this world. A person who lives her life in compassion for all of life is a gift indeed.

Often times the word compassion is confused with the word sympathy. Although these two words are similar there is also a great difference. One who lives in sympathy feels for the other person and actually gets into the space or energy of what another is going through, taking on the sadness of the other person. It's like stepping into the other person's shoes. Although their intention may be genuine they only add their own sorrow to it. When this occurs it is not helping another but hindering that person's own healing and growth process.

A compassionate person is filled with an innate wisdom and understands what another person is going through. It is a feeling of unselfish tenderness towards a person in need. You take yourself out of judgment about a person or situation to be of service to another human being. You act out of the kindness of your own heart.

To carry this divine trait you must learn to think well of yourself and others. Sometimes being compassionate means standing in the integrity of your heart and helping others to see their own strengths or weaknesses. This could mean you are understanding when one is coming from the "Oh poor me" syndrome, but to explain to them out of the compassion of your heart that they are not a victim of any circumstance. That is an act of compassion, helping others to understand the truth.

I can relate to a situation that occurred within a circle of long-time acquaintances where the most compassionate thing I could do was to stand in my truth and say to this person that I was not willing to listen to his negativity anymore. I, of course, did not say it this bluntly but that is what the bottom line of the message conveyed. I tried to explain how fortunate and loved this person was and that he needed to dwell on the positive instead of the negative. If I had continued to keep listening to this person plant negative seeds about how unhappy he was with everyone and everything then I would have done a great disservice to him, myself, and to all the ones that were complained about. It didn't mean I loved him any less, but he needed to see how he affected those around him. For many years I observed everyone always sidestep and ignore the situation. No one would ever approach this person about his behavior for fear of the anger and wrath that could result from it. But how are people going to start shifting their awareness if we always leave it up to someone else? This was a very difficult situation for me because I knew what the consequences could be. My only intention was to get him to see how blessed he was in this life and to start seeing the good qualities in everyone and everything. I was willing to risk the interaction and reaction this person would display and willing to let him go in love if no resolve was made.

Let's take a look at how compassionate you are. When someone is hurting or feeling bad, do you merely say, "I'm so sorry that happened to you," and on you go? Do you simply say, "That's too bad. Let me know if there is anything I can do." and you are on your way? Or do you truly try to be of some help to them? Do you sit with them and try to understand their situation and offer understanding and nonjudgmental help? Is there a payoff if you help them? Or are you helping them from the goodness of your heart? If there is reason or payoff behind helping someone then it is not compassion but selfishness. In compassion there is a genuine caring and value you have for another human being. It has nothing to do with whether or not they will be able to repay you later.

The word sorry means sad or unhappy, and of course there are appropriate times to use "I'm sorry." For the most part this terminology is a very common but misunderstood statement that should be used with great discretion. It often comes in the form of sympathy when it should not be intended as such. Being sorry for someone is usually only adding the energy of sadness or unhappiness to a situation. Instead, be in compassion for the other person and tell them, "I understand what you are going through, how you must feel, the immensity of your challenge…" These two words, "I understand", allow you to step into the energy of compassion with each person instead of the energy of sadness, anger, etc.. This also gives the person you are talking to a much deeper understanding that you truly do have his best interest in mind. There is a very subtle difference between "I'm sorry" and "I understand", but a huge difference in how it can bring a more uplifting energy to almost any situation.

The feeling of compassion is profound. In true compassion your heart lives in its integrity, your thoughts are pure and uplifting. You live in love for all humankind, and with your offering of true compassion to any situation you will receive love back in untold measure.

Become the embodiment of this great virtue. Let compassion envelop and bathe your heart. It is a virtue that is developed from within. Continually ask God for the grace to feel more and more compassionate towards everyone. When you become the embodiment of compassion, wherever you go, people will know they will receive your help. They will feel safe and secure in your presence because you carry within you an incredible tenderness of the heart.

Inspiration Exercises

- Write down two examples where you gave sympathy to someone, where you really got into their stuff and started to feel bad with them, actually taking on some of their sorrow, hurt, anger, or other feelings.

  Now write down two incidences where you gave compassion to someone, where you stood in your heart but did not allow yourself to get caught up in the other person's drama. You came from a point of understanding, giving them support, helping them to perhaps see things in a different light.

  Examine the differences between sympathy and compassion in both of these circumstances. When you were in sympathy how did you feel? How did you feel when you were in compassion? Begin to discern the subtle and not so subtle differences in how it affects you and the other person.

- This is a great exercise to practice. Note how many times each day this week you say, "Oh, I'm so sorry that this or that happened to you." In the evening write down several of the instances in which you said, "I'm sorry." Now write the day's incidents from an "I understand perspective". Begin to discern the difference between the two and which one you truly meant. Practice using this different expression and change your verbiage when it is appropriate.

- Write down a situation in which the most compassionate thing you could have done for someone was to stand in your truth and tell a person something that was very difficult for them to hear and for you to tell, but you knew it would help that individual grow. How did this feel? Was it difficult?

Did you feel like you were in compassion at the time? Was the information given with great love? Can you understand now how it could be considered compassion when looking at it from a higher perspective if the information was given from a standpoint of love?

If you cannot think of an example where you have done this, begin to review a situation you are presently going through and how you could now deal with it in a compassionate way.

CHAPTER 7

Does Your Heart Live in Humility?

Humility is the rarest of rare attainments and is not all that easily achieved. It takes a very courageous heart to become humble.

Humility needs to be intricately woven within and around the heart and if it is, it will definitely lead you to the heart of God. Baba Muktananda, a great Indian saint once stated, "In your worldly life, people may be impressed by your family or by other external factors. But, as far as God is concerned, He pays absolutely no attention to your body, to its beauty, or to your facial features. He doesn't pay attention to your sense organs. He only values the feelings in your heart."

To be humble is to neither seek nor expect credit for your actions. For most people even if they perform a tiny little deed they want the whole world to hear about it. Humility takes continual self-inquiry as to your purpose behind every thought, word and action. For what purpose do you give? What space are you coming from when you give? Are you performing your actions from your heart or is it for a reward? The same principle applies for thoughts and words.

There is a remarkable philanthropic organization in the city in which I live. They seek out and review remarkable acts of compassion that have occurred during the year and vote for the one that is the most extraordinary. This award is for someone who has gone above and beyond the call of duty in helping other human beings in distress. This organization tracks the heroic person down and explains they want to honor her at a dinner affair and give them a special award. I have been told by this organization that although there are many incredible kind and noble acts of compassion that happen during any given year, it is difficult to get the people who performed them to want to receive credit for their actions. Some are even astonished that they would be chosen for what they did. They have insisted anyone would have done the same thing or that they don't feel they need to be rewarded because they were just trying to be helpful.

The next time you do something nice for someone don't tell a soul about it no matter how great your effort was. As you may be aware, every thought, word and action is recorded in the skeins of time, but don't even do these acts of kindness for the merits of heaven. Just take care of others. See how humble you can be. Perform your actions without motive or reward. Let it be a secret between you and God. The infinite treasures of heaven await those who have humbleness of the heart.

Inspiration Exercises

- Write down the names of one or two people you feel who are humble. What does it mean to be humble? What makes them humble? What are the characteristics of those who shows humility in their life? What makes them special? Are these the type of individuals you like to be around and why? This is a great practice because humbleness can be such a subtle virtue you may be overlooking simple everyday acts of humbleness that others display.

- Go back in your memory and look at three fairly large instances in which you helped someone. How many people did you tell of your act of kindness or heroism so they knew how generous or outstanding you were? A good example is of a football quarterback who made the winning touchdown 10 years ago and he is still talking about it today. All of you know people like this.

- Do at least one act of kindness each day this week and tell no one. Can you do this? Of course I can, you say. It is so simple. For example, if someone drops her keys on the floor and you pick them up you probably never think twice about it. But let's say that today you went to your supervisor's boss and told him how wonderful you felt your supervisor was because you want to acknowledge the work and good example she sets for the staff. Can you keep it a secret or would you afterwards be telling your supervisor what you did for her if for nothing more than just telling her to make her feel good. This, of course, would make you look good also. Perhaps you may tell your supervisor what you did but you have ulterior motives in mind in hopes that you will receive a raise or get extra time off when you need it. In other words, was there a payoff for you? Think about your acts of kindness and the humility that is or is not a part of your action. Do all acts of kindness with no thought of reward other than the realization that you can thank God you had the ability to be able to offer what you have or can give to others.

CHAPTER 8

Does Your Heart Live in Wisdom?

I always thought I was wise. Didn't you always think you were wise? In my twenties I thought I knew everything. It was the same story when I entered my thirties and forties and so on. However, with each passing decade I was beginning to learn that I had not been as wise at 20 as I now was at 30. When I turned 40, I realized I was not as wise as I thought I was at 30. Do I need to go on? The older you are the more you will resonate with what I am stating. I've watched this repeated in my children and I now just stand back and smile, just like my parents did with me.

How does one live in wisdom, let alone live in the wisdom of the heart? On a very intellectual level, wisdom can be described as using the good discrimination in dealing with all people and things. It is based on life experiences, knowledge, and understanding.

Why we think we know it all by 20, when our life is just beginning, I will never understand. There is a certain amount of life experiences that one has to accumulate to truly understand what life is all about and these are things that only time can give. Now that I'm in my fifties I'm realizing the more I think I know the less I do know. Maybe that's good. There is a certain amount of wisdom that evolves over time as one goes through life living through good times, bad times, and in-between times. When we are confronted with a situation we can draw upon this storehouse of knowledge and share our experiences even if it is only from our perception.

Then again I have seen very mature adults with a lot of life experiences, who are incredibly intelligent, but do not work from a point of wisdom in any way, shape, or form. So let's look at another aspect of what truly makes any person wise no matter what his age. This requires a much deeper understanding of where true wisdom comes from. First there is a knowledge factor. It is a knowing that wisdom is the result of searching deep within one's own being for the truth. There is a still small voice within that is always ready to help you act from the deep wellspring of wisdom within the heart. Drop into this space and ask for guidance. Stop and think from this space. It is often called intuition or a sixth sense. From this heart space rises feelings and knowledge of what is the right action to take and what should be said. The more you drop into this space the more the gift of clear thinking arises and your judgment improves. You begin to see people through the eyes of love and compassion as you begin to recognize the God in everyone and everything. This is true wisdom.

Most people are so busy with what is going on in their outer lives, or so concerned about the opinions of others, or so filled with the clutter of the mind and rushing from here to there that they never venture to the inner realms. They never explore the depths of their hearts for answers. No time is spent in dropping into that heart space to think about what they are saying or doing. They just act in the moment without thought of the consequences. A person of wisdom listens within and then reacts, always taking into account his experience and trying to deal with all situations in the highest way possible.

Does Your Heart Live in Wisdom?

Here is a story about a foster teen that I had at one point in my life. It relays an act of simple wisdom at a young age and I think you will enjoy it. He was seventeen at the time and one of the most delightful young people I knew even with skull rings on every finger and a Mohawk haircut. The police came knocking at my door not long after he moved in and wanted to know where he was. It had been reported that he broke into a car at the high school and stole a very expensive snowboard from the trunk of one of the students. I will skip all the details of this escapade, but eventually he returned the snowboard and did community service to pay for his actions.

While all this was going on, I sat down with him to explain the laws of karma, and how every action has a reaction, how and what you do to others always comes back now, or in the future or in another lifetime, but you will have something that you value taken from you. This is how the universe works. Then I told him that if he wanted a snowboard, he should get a job and earn the money to buy one (a new concept for him!). We got him started back to school (he had dropped out) and he took my bit of wisdom and got a part-time job. Not much time passed and he was able to work out the differences with his parents and he moved back home. One day several months later I was at work going up an escalator when he came bounding up behind me to say hello. He said, "Hi Julie, Look at this." He pushed something in front of my eyes that appeared to look like a sales receipt but before I could really examine it he blurted out in great exuberance, "I bought my own snowboard. It cost $450 and I paid for it with the money I earned from my job." I was so excited for him and proud of him too. I instantly began to tell him so, but he stopped me and said, "But wait that's not all. Guess what? It was stolen! How is that for almost instant karma for ya?" We both laughed for a few seconds and then I asked him how he felt about the whole thing. He said that he had really taken to heart what I had said about karma and understood what had happened. He was now trying to live in a higher awareness of his actions. He had no remorse because he felt like he had just paid off a debt. He may not have realized it but he was actually coming from a deep point of the wisdom of the heart, that what you give is what you receive. By the way his hands were free of rings and his hair was trimmed.

Let the wisdom of your heart shine forth. As you begin your day drop into your heart and ask God to work through you for the best and highest good of everyone so that all your actions, words and thoughts may come from the wisdom of the heart. Just by doing this and becoming aware of your actions you will become wiser with each passing day.

Inspiration Exercises

May every word you say be said as if everyone in the world could hear it, for in fact they can.

♥ Yesterday is but a memory yet still fresh in your mind and heart. Take yesterday's events and pick several instances when you may or may not have dropped into the wisdom of the heart in dealing with someone. Examine the situations and look at how you reacted. Did you make a flip comment to someone? Did you come from sarcasm or teasing? Was it a quick response you later regretted? Did you think how a statement you may have made affected the person who received it? How would you have received it? Today and for the rest of the week hesitate just a moment before you speak and let the words that roll off of the tongue come from the love of the heart, the innate wisdom of that divine space.

May every thought that you think be etched in fire in the sky for the whole world to see, for indeed it is.

May every wish that you wish another be a wish that you wish for yourself, because in fact it is.

♥ Perhaps you never encountered another soul yesterday or you were surrounded by a myriad of individuals. Delve into yesterday's thought patterns and look at what was foremost on your mind. Even our thoughts come from a point of wisdom or non-wisdom. Were your thoughts positive or negative? Was your self-talk uplifting or degrading? Did you wish the best for someone else who may have wronged you, or did you send them love? We have power over our thoughts just as we do our words.

The Heart: The Final Destination

Now review several of these thought patterns and how you could have changed yesterday's self talk to make it higher. Rerun the incident in your mind and practice this new thought pattern five times for every situation.

- ♥ Now, as usually happens, the situation that was at the forefront of your mind yesterday is usually still there today. Our minds are like a cassette tape that is on continual rewind and replay, repeating over and over again something that is bothering us. Every time that problem or challenge or situation drifts through your thought process, even if it is a hundred times a day, instead of it being a negative, sad or depressing thought, use the positive thought that you have practiced to replace the negative feeling. This will change the energy of not only the situation but the feeling itself over time. This does not happen overnight, but with practice. What higher offering could you give anyone or anything except to have positive thoughts?

- ♥ The first thing in the morning when you get out of bed and then during the day - over and over, offer your thoughts, words, and actions to God. Write yourself post-it notes to remind yourself: "I think the highest thoughts", "I speak with love", "All my actions are the highest", "I offer all my thoughts, words and actions to God." Put the notes everywhere. It not only makes you feel good seeing them but practicing will connect you with the deeper innate wisdom of the heart and will be a constant reminder of tapping into the power of this wisdom.

CHAPTER 9

Does Your Heart Live in Patience?

Lord, give me patience, and do it right now! For most of my life this has been my motto and this has to be one of my greatest lessons to learn. Over the years I have made great progress in this department but I really do work at keeping myself in check. I think that of all the virtues, this one, not only for me, but for most everyone, is probably one of the number one lessons to be learned in the world today.

Patience is a noble quality and an extraordinary practice. Living in patience is an expression of great freedom and strength. What is patience? In order to understand patience let's look at what it is not - impatience. Do you ever question why you become impatient? What makes you lose patience with yourself, others, and situations? For most of us it is because we have our own agenda about how things should be or what time lengths they should be done in. We have preconceived ideas that do not match up with what actually happens. These are our desires. When our own desires are not met, what happens? We get angry and have dropped out of patience.

Think about a project that is due on a date you had arbitrarily set and the goal is not met. You lose your patience. Or maybe you've told your three-year-old a zillion times not to play in the mud puddles and she still does. You lose your patience. The car in front of you isn't in a hurry like you are. You lose your patience. You have put your own time lines in place, your own desires for when something should be accomplished or learned. When these desires are thwarted, you get angry and lose your patience.

Here are some more examples. How about when you're rushing to get things done? You trip and stub your toe, run into doors, forget important papers, or lose things and then it takes twice as long to set things right, or you stand there wasting more time holding your toe because it hurts too much to walk on, when if you had just gone a little slower you wouldn't have tripped. It usually turns out that if you had been patient to begin with you would have saved more time. These instances are about living deliberately, taking the time to take the time. In other words, being patient.

What about the day-in-day-out chores you rush through as quickly as possible so you can go on to your next task? And then rush through that task and then rush through the next task. Pretty soon you have rushed right through the entire day. This completely takes the joy out of living. When this happens, you sacrifice the quality and beauty of each endeavor. When you take the time to complete a task with patience you are honoring and respecting the process of what you are trying to accomplish. Have you noticed how different you feel when you rush through a project than if you think it through and thoughtfully, deliberately, and patiently complete it? Don't you feel better and more relaxed? Even so-called mundane chores can be fun if you put the time and care into them that they deserve. There really is no such thing as a mundane chore. After all, aren't you mopping the kitchen floor to make it a welcoming and clean place to cook in and enjoy with your family?

Aren't you cleaning the windows to honor the beauty of the sun coming through to light your home?

Now I know you have probably been told this a dozen times but I'm going to say it anyway. Never, never get in your car without a magazine, a book, project, stationery, unread mail that is stacking up - whatever. Always take something to do in case you end up in a line or traffic jam somewhere. I have left my house to drive two blocks to do the most simple of simple errands (I should have walked but I was in a hurry!) and have gotten stuck in traffic that took an hour to get out of, and this place wasn't even a busy street! You just never know. And yes, I had stationery and a notepad. I was able to complete my grocery list and write several overdue letters to some friends. This definitely helps with the patience quotient.

If you have to leave a sticky note on your front door for awhile to get into the habit of remembering to take something with you to do in case you are stuck somewhere, then do it. You will feel so much better for not having wasted time. In our busy lives we need to feel our time is being used wisely and productively. It is important. By always having something to do you will have honored precious time no matter where you are, and your blood pressure will stay stable.

Today I had a lunch meeting with a client at a restaurant and we were both coming from about 20 miles away. I instinctively grabbed some of my stacked up mail to take with me just in case the person I was meeting was late. Sure enough they were, by about 10 minutes, and it was perfect for me. I got caught up on miscellaneous reading, which I never seem to do at home.

If one practices the patience of the heart diligently, one is rewarded with the gift of patience itself. Life is too short not to be patient. Be a little bit more lenient and gentle with your desires. If they are not met then give a little, sometimes a lot. Everything happens in its own time and all the impatience in the world will not make things happen faster. That is just the way it is.

This magnificent and noble quality of patience is a gem that exists in your heart. It is your birthright. To shine forth it must be polished through and through with continual practice. Be slow to anger in this world and learn to live in patience. This creates great freedom in your life and you will find your life will begin to take on a new meaning. As you step into patience, it will bring you closer to your heart. Everyone will love you for it.

Inspiration Exercises

- ❤ Think of a time when you were rushed and stressed to meet a deadline. Did it do you any good to rush, perhaps putting others in danger if you needed to drive somewhere? Did it really matter if you were a few minutes late? And if it did, then could you have planned your day better so you did not have to rush? What about a project you knew about for a month and kept putting off until the last minute emergency came up, and then you were really stressing out for lack of time? What about your two year old crying, your six year old wanting attention, and you trying to make dinner all at the same time? You begin to lose your patience. How could you handle this differently? I invite you to take several instances that have stressed you out where there appeared to be a lack of time, then be creative to see how you could have met the needs that need to be met and still maintain your patience. Even just stopping to take a few deep breaths can do wonders.

- ❤ Be patient with yourself, allow yourself to plan ahead. If this is not a habit of yours, try this for several days and see the results of planning your day. Set a plan in the morning or the night before and stick to it, allowing enough time for changes to occur. I always offer my day to God and then in prayer I explain what I have planned for that day. Then I ask for blessings to accomplish what I have planned and if God has other plans for me I ask for the blessings and grace to do that instead. I finish with, "I align my will with the will of God." This allows me the space to be content no matter what happens.

The Heart: The Final Destination

- ❤ SLOW DOWN! Take one task, one mundane chore, and very patiently take the time to do it deliberately and consciously. Actually think about what you are doing and do not let your mind wander. As you are vacuuming the carpet, mowing the yard, repairing a bicycle, washing the car, fixing dinner - keep thinking about doing whatever you are doing the very best way you can. Know it is a loving gesture to honor those you live with, yourself, friends, possessions, whomever or whatever. Allow your heart do each chore instead of your mind. Give yourself to whatever you do completely. After you have done this, then take the time to reflect on how you felt when you took the time to give patience and focus to a simple task. It's almost like a huge sigh of relief. Just try it. Keep increasing the number of tasks you apply this principle to. This exercise is not as easy as it sounds but with practice it becomes a way of life and helps develop the sought after virtue of patience.

- ❤ Gather that extra stationery, favorite magazine, this book, and keep it in your vehicle just in case you get caught in a traffic jam. This will help your patience quota immensely.

- ❤ The next time you have to stand in a line or are in a standstill on the freeway, instead of becoming frustrated start sending blessings to everyone instead. And remember to breathe deeply.

CHAPTER 10

Does Your Heart Live in Gentleness?

"Nothing is so strong as gentleness, nothing so gentle as real strength." This is a beautiful quote by a French saint that I have heard many times in my life and it is worth contemplating deeply. People who exhibit the benevolent rays of gentleness allow you to feel loved. True gentleness touches your heart and you feel at peace.

What would a world of true gentleness feel like? Doesn't everyone appreciate being welcomed with gentleness? Nothing seems so comforting when you are sad as a gentle hug from a friend or when you are sick, a soothing word of caring and concern. Do you know of anyone who ever complains of you being too gentle?

To begin to feel the gentleness of your heart start with one of the greatest gifts God gave us, the gentleness of nature. Let your heart drop into the gentleness of the sunrise as it beckons us forth to begin a new day, the gentle moonbeams reflecting off a still clear lake at night, or the gentle unfolding of a delicate flower during the day. Feel the soft gentle breeze as it floats through the leaves of the trees or feel the gentle magical mist of a light fog as it embraces your being while walking along the ocean shore. These are all examples of the beauty of nature's gentleness.

Another one of nature's gifts is the gentleness of animals. See the gentle look in your pet's eyes or listen to the gentle purr of a kitty as you stroke its fur. The gentle innocent look of baby animals is so appealing you want to drop whatever you are doing just to be with them. Think how deliberately, gently and carefully you would pick up a baby bird or a baby panda. We need to learn to walk the earth with the awareness of this deliberate gentleness.

What about being gentle with yourself? You will make mistakes, blunders, do things you later regret, and things you literally wish you could crawl under a rug and hide from for the rest of your life. But guess what?, life goes on and your destiny continues to unfold. How do you deal with these awkward incidents in life? Be gentle with yourself. Don't berate yourself but look at every incident with the eye of gentleness, forgive yourself, learn from it, be wiser for it, offer love to it, and on you go. That gentleness in dealing with yourself is exactly what God wants you to do.

Gentleness lives in the heart but it must be cultivated. It won't come forward and shine if it is not cultivated. So many people put up a tough front because they are afraid to step into this divine virtue. Have you ever worked for someone who believes that his way is the only way? They outwardly show that they are in control and that everyone better tow the line. It would probably be wiser to ask who hasn't worked for someone of this nature? These types of people feel that only through total control will the work get done. They feel that if they work from a point of gentleness they will get walked on and taken advantage of. However, if they don't learn to step into this realm of gentleness, they are doing nothing but creating unhappiness and fear in all around them.

It takes courage to be gentle with others. Now if you're one of those bosses who leads with an iron fist, I'm not talking about giving your power away. I'm talking about shifting it to a different way of operating. You can be powerful and gentle at the same time. If you can learn to be gentle with your employees, cultivate their good qualities, get to know them, truly care about them, incorporate their ideas, and encourage them from a standpoint of true gentleness then you will have a team that will back you up and take care of you too. Think about a time when someone has dealt with you in gentleness. Didn't you feel filled with gratitude? The key here is that you, the boss, have to start. It comes from the top down. If the boss is gentle it allows others to blossom and be gentle also. Model what you seek others to follow.

To work from a point of gentleness does not mean that you become a pushover at the mercy of any little circumstance that comes along. There needs to exist a fine line of harmony and balance. You are not meant to be as soft as butter, ready to melt in an instant, nor are you meant to be as hard as steel, not bending or yielding. Do every action with the intent of gentleness, of acting in the highest interest of everyone. Create this balance so gentleness can come to the forefront in your dealings with everyone.

I can tell you this. If you are not gentle and caring with your staff, they are probably working out of fear. And when someone is working out of fear they are not giving you a 100 percent and really don't care to. Why would they? They will do what they need to get by to get that paycheck; and when a better job comes along, they will eventually leave you. But, if you change your attitude and begin to come from gentleness of being, of truly caring about each one of them, then your staff will love you and work twice as hard and will want to be on your team.

I once had a job for several years where the turnover in management happened quite often. This was just the nature of this particular occupation because of managers wanting to move up the corporate ladder which would happen rather quickly. Consequently, the choice of managers was not always thought through and there was little if any management training to help the new managers learn people skills or how to take care of their staff. There were many times I observed a staff go from being happy, liking what they were doing, feeling heard and cared about, producing high-quality work and with great production statistics; to living in fear, closing down, feeling they were just a number, angry at their new manager and the company, with a decline in production and quality of work. This was always a result of a new manager coming in who believed in controlling people out of fear and being unbending and lacking in compassion because they just didn't know any better. They felt they had to show everyone who was in command. This particular type of manager never did last long. Thank goodness. Can you imagine what the turnover rate of employees were for this company?

Where do you stand in treating others with gentleness? Do you have the courage to ask your staff how they feel about you? And if you do, will they tell you the truth? Not if they live in fear of you, they won't. To be courageous enough to enter into the gentleness of the heart may be one of the biggest steps in your life. Just do it. It takes practice but it will not only benefit you, but the lives of everyone around you, too.

When you are an employer, parent or anyone with authority, convey gentleness to others. When you are able to speak with gentleness and act from gentleness, it creates love and removes fear. And doesn't everyone want to feel loved? Doesn't everyone want to be free from fear? When you act from this premise of gentleness it also takes _your_ fear away and helps to open _your_ heart. Gentleness, allows you to trust others and helps you to move forward. You begin to relax and see the innate goodness in everyone and in the universe. This type of gentleness is a strength that comes from your heart.

Do you begin to see that when you feel gentle it's not about feeling weak? You stand in the truth of your heart. The strength of your caring and supporting of others is actually the gentleness of your heart shining forth.

"Nothing is so strong as gentleness, nothing so gentle as real strength."

Inspiration Exercises

- ♥ Take one hour each day this week and practice this trait of gentleness. First of all sit quietly for a few minutes and repeat to yourself, "I am gentle in all my actions. It takes someone truly strong to be gentle and I am strong, therefore I am also gentle. Because I am strong I face my day with the power of gentleness and my actions reflect a gentle nature." Then take the next hour and genuinely practice gentleness in every action whether it is with your family, workers, or friends. Keep practicing and increasing the time you allow yourself to step into this virtue. It will pay off a hundredfold in your life.

- ♥ Now take any task, following the above instructions, and do the same. For example, if you are going to finish building your garage today, treat your tools gently - it is a gift that you have them, handle the wood with gentleness - with the awareness that a tree gave its life so you could build something to protect your possessions. Or as you prepare your food for dinner treat each item with gentleness and offer love to all who helped get it to you, the earth, farms, transport system, grocery store, etc. This exercise can be done with absolutely any task, simple to complex.

- ♥ Reflect in your mind two separate occasions when you stepped out of gentleness and into fear, anger, blame, or frustration with a loved one or co-worker. Write them down and rerun the situation in your mind to how you could have perhaps dealt with these instances in a firm but gentle manner. As you write your answers on paper, forgive yourself for originally not coming from a gentle manner. This allows a releasing of energy to occur and helps to heal situations. Doesn't this give the feeling of honoring the situation and the other person? Through practicing this exercise you will become aware of when you are not treating others with the gentleness that comes from strength, and you will eventually incorporate gentleness into all your future interactions.

- ♥ For parents, children can push our buttons more easily than anything I can think of. How often do you see gentleness lacking in the way parents treat their children? A lot. How many times have you witnessed parents interacting with their child and you are thinking, "I would never want her/him for a parent." You are looking at the situation from the standpoint of a child and this is good. What would it feel like to be the child, that child that is so very vulnerable? Remember that as these children grow up they model their parents and will do the same if not more to their own children. We need to treat our children not out of fear, control and command, but with firmness, gentleness and a lot of love. Take one hour every day and practice firmness and gentleness in your actions with your children. Before doing it take a minute or two to go inside and repeat the affirmation in the first exercise so you are in the right space and then interact with your children from that point of love, firmness, and above all gentleness. Watch them begin to flourish under your loving care.

CHAPTER 11

Does Your Heart Live in Gratitude?

How many of us take our lives for granted? I know I did for years. A lot of us go through our lifetime and never think twice about having food, clothing, shelter, and any of the finer things in life. Our parents' provided for us in one way or another and we eventually transitioned out of our parents' homes as we grew up and started collecting things of our own. Although it may have been challenging at times we slowly acquired our own home or apartment, three televisions, four phones, two cars, stereos, VCRs, and on and on the list goes. At least this was close to my upbringing; so many material things we seem to think we need.

People would talk about gratitude but because I had been so fortunate in my youth in receiving material things and never having lost anyone close to me, I couldn't really grasp the concept of what it would be like to go without loved ones or material abundance — and who wants to try that? We usually don't go about seeking emptiness and poverty.

I ended up with a job when I was fairly young that taught me at a very deep level what gratitude was all about, and I started to look at things differently, but where I truly learned to be grateful was when I moved to India. For two years I lived in an ashram (a monastery) with one of the greatest living masters of our age. The ashram was about two and a half hours out of Bombay, and once a week I had to travel into this city of thirteen million people where the poverty was overwhelming. The episode I am about to share changed my life forever. It was one of those moments in time that the heart never forgets and even as I type it I start to weep because it touched my heart to its very core.

Poverty abounds in this city. At first it is such a shock that the mind goes numb. You begin to feel that this cannot be real and so the mind sort of puts up its own blinders. You begin to adopt the concept that this is just a movie set that you somehow are viewing. Even though I would protect myself with my own mindset, I would keep my heart open and continually send blessings. Poverty is such a way of life there and after a while you adjust to it because it begins to seem so natural. Life goes on and one just goes about doing his business, just stepping around it and over it all. I stepped over people sleeping on streets, dead rats and animals, huge unprotected open manholes in sidewalks and tripped over snake baskets with cobras.

But one scene that I observed several times while I was on the shuttle as we would enter Bombay proper was one I shall never forget, and it took gratitude to another whole dimension for me. It was a young street girl about ten years of age and she was walking on this filthy sidewalk using her two hands and one good leg. Her other leg was dragging along the sidewalk behind her because she had a deformed foot. She had on a dress that was tattered, torn and filthy which was dragging on the ground in the front as she limped along like a dog with three legs. The shuttle I was on would sometimes stop at the light so I was able to watch her as she tried to maneuver herself along.

After closley observing her several times it was quite plain to see that her deformity could have been resolved with medical treatment and surgery. This youngster also could have walked had she had a simple pair of crutches. At this point the way she walked had become her lifestyle and would probably remain so until she died. This is just the way it is there. My heart ached for this young one. I would always try to put it into a logical perspective for myself because I do know that in India these birth defects also work to an advantage for a family. It makes it easier for them to be beggars because they have living proof they need money. This, however, is at the expense of another human beings' life. "But for the grace of God, it could be me."

I remember being told to even be grateful if someone gives you a pinch of salt. Be grateful that you can hold a glass of water in your hand. That in itself is a miracle. Be grateful you have eyes to see your children. Be grateful you have a hand to feel the fur of your beloved pet. I began to start counting my blessings with a heart full of gratitude for all I had been given in this life. If I began today and did nothing for the rest of my life but count my blessings, I could never finish if I lived to be a hundred.

Take this for example. Right now observe the room in which you are sitting and look around. How long would it take you to thank God for every single item there? Even for the carpet or linoleum that protects your feet, or the walls or the paint that makes the walls beautiful and colorful, for the windows that let in the light, or the chair that allows you to sit on it. What about the tree that gave up its life so you could sit in that chair? We should remember that everything we have or use is actually a gift. We can't really own anything. You could lose everything you own in an earthquake or a flood this afternoon. Nor can you take anything with you when you die. If you can lose things this easily, what makes you think it is exclusively yours to begin with? So think of every item that you have as a gift, whether you purchased it or not, and give thanks for it. One never knows what the day will bring.

Here is a more uplifting and heartfelt account of gratitude. Several years ago several Hawaiian islands were in the path of a major hurricane. The people had several hours to prepare for its coming and everyone on this particular island were told to evacuate their homes. They could bring any valuable items they could carry and come to the huge hotel near the bay to stay in the basement where it was the safest place on the island to be during the storm.

This one particular lady lived alone and had a beautiful home. She had great understanding of life and was aware that in the higher scheme of things she did not truly own this home even though she had purchased it and was making payments on it. She was always filled with gratitude for having this lovely home and felt it was a gift from God, a place that had been loaned to her during this lifetime. She kept her home clean and neat, but when she heard of the deadly potential of this hurricane, and that it was headed straight for the island she lived on, she made an amazing decision. Instead of rushing around in a panic trying to decide what valuables to save she decided she would not give in to fear but honor her home and prepare it to offer it back to God.

So she cleaned her entire home with great love and then, before she left her home for the last time, she went through every room and thanked it for giving her such joy and protection for so many years. Having given thanks, she offered her house back to God and stated that it was His will to do with it as He pleased. She then walked out of her house with just a few clothes and some important papers and went to the hotel.

The hurricane hit and the short-wave radio reports they were receiving in the basement of this hotel stated that everything in the area had been destroyed and that it was declared a national emergency disaster area. When it was deemed safe, everyone slowly filtered out of the hotel through the rubble and fallen palms to trek by foot to see what was left of their previous homes, to see what, if anything, they could salvage. This lady was fully prepared to see an empty space where her house had stood, but instead what she saw was unbelievable. While everyone's house had been completely demolished, her home was the only one standing, totally intact. It had barely been touched by the winds. She was so filled with gratitude that she opened her home to all who could be accommodated. This home became a major refuge to the less fortunate as they began to put their lives back together.

Every day, every hour, every minute of your existence remain focused on the grace that sustains you, and with all your heart feel gratitude for what you have been given. Take a minute or two each day to give thanks for what you have no matter how little it may seem. Pretty soon you will realize how fortunate you are just to be alive, and to hold that glass of water in your hand.

Gratitude is a great state to live in and it makes your life feel like it is the most precious gift in the world. If you were to pick only one exercise from this book to practice on a routine basis, this should be it. A heart that lives in gratitude is worth all the precious gems in the world.

Inspiration Exercises

- ♥ Put yourself in the position of the woman in Hawaii who had just been told a hurricane was directly headed for her home. Do this with your own home. What would it be like to lose everything you supposedly thought you owned? If you lost everything today, which some of you have, what would you do? How would you feel? Deep pain, sorrow, frustration, sadness and anger are all natural feelings that could come up, but what about gratitude? Does gratitude well up in your heart for all you have been given to know that everything was a gift and now the universe is allowing something new to enter your life to help you grow? Did you appreciate the home and items you had when you had them? How filled with gratitude are you for all your belongings?

- ♥ Take ten minutes every day for five days, pick a different room each day in your home or apartment. Sit down and become still inside. As your eyes gently shut and you become quiet, begin to mentally go through each item in that room and give thanks that you are so fortunate to be blessed with its presence. Look at how that item has served you with entertainment, safety, warmth, joy or sustenance. Now take the other two days left in the week and go into nature and repeat the same exercise. Then take a moment to thank your car for the protection it has given you, how it has kept you warm or cool, provided you with beautiful music from its radio and responded to your every whim. Can you begin to see how so very blessed you are? All of these gifts are right before your eyes, and through the continual practice of gratitude you will be astounded at what you have taken for granted day after day, year after year, and your heart will begin to open wide.

Does Your Heart Live in Gratitude?

- ♥ Take three people that are very important to you in this life and reflect on how and why you love them and why they mean so much to you. Commit your answers to paper. What have they done for you that you love them so much? What characteristics do they show you that endears them to you? Mentally thank them for being in your life and tell them why. Now get together with those individuals and tell them in person or on the phone how and why you are filled with gratitude to be a part of their lives, and that they are a part of yours.

CHAPTER 12

Does Your Heart Live in Enthusiasm?

Don't you just love to be around people who are enthusiastic and in love with life and everyone and everything around them? It's as if these people see the awe and wonder in life and are always ready to celebrate whatever comes their way. Aren't these the people you automatically gravitate to? If you walk in a room and see one person with a frown on his or her face and one with a smile, which one would you want to sit by? If you had a choice to talk to someone who is angry, unhappy, and vindictive, or someone who is cheerful, joyous and positive, which would be your choice? Our hearts and entire being gravitate to the light, don't they?

Enthusiasm makes your whole life soar. The seed of enthusiasm that dwells within your heart is always ready to blossom forth. So how does one begin to be enthusiastic about life? It begins by living in awe and wonder at the simplest of things, by being enthusiastic about something so simple as a grain of sand. We must step into a continual feeling of abundance in our life no matter what happens, and to live deliberately in every moment. From these small acts of enthusiasm about simple things, you will find that enthusiasm begins to grow and starts to encompass bigger things, and then eventually all of life.

I'll never forget an incident that occurred when I was in charge of an art department several years ago. There were six very talented artists and the work they put out amazed me. This one particular artist could paint in almost any medium and turned out exquisite detailed work. One day I received a card in the mail and it was one of those rudementary cards from India, or at least that is what I thought at the time. I read it, appreciated receiving it, and was going to throw it away when this one particular artist I admired so much happened to be walking by and enthusiastically started talking about how beautiful the drawing on this card was. She was in such awe and wonder of this simple piece of work. I looked at it again and said, "You have got to be kidding. This is so simple, a five year old could have done it. It can't begin to compare to your work. What do you see in it?" She said, "No, no, you don't understand. This is just a different kind of art and the person that drew this was doing the very best they knew how. I think it's beautiful." She was literally ooh-ing and ah-ing over it as she explained why she thought it was so amazing. I just about fell out of my chair! She was such an accomplished artist, yet her enthusiasm for even this simple, what I thought to be a thrown together piece of art threw me off balance.

I thought about my reaction to this card because I had always really valued this other person's judgment. This is how she lived her life, in awe and wonder of everything - enthusiastic about everything. Obviously I was in judgment. After I got over my initial shock, I was embarrassed that I didn't see the beauty in the card that she did. It really made me stop and think, so much so that I took the card home that night and contemplated what this event was all about for me. In something I saw as mundane she saw only beauty. As they say, beauty is in the eye of the beholder. I don't know how it happened, but as I was contemplating something inside of me clicked, and all of a sudden my heart opened wide to the wonder and beauty in this drawing and then it broadened into a panorama of the beauty in all things. This was a seed for the start of another level of great enthusiasm that began to unfold in my life.

Now I had always felt as if I were an enthusiastic person, and I think most everyone who knew me would have said the same thing, but this one incident put a whole different level of understanding into my concept of enthusiasm. It was as if I had awakened from a slumber from which I didn't know I had been sleeping. All of a sudden I was in awe of everything. I was in awe of the marble floor beneath my feet and began to be in awe as to how the earth made it, how it was taken from the earth, what process did it have to go through to be made so shiny, the people that brought it here, the people who laid it, and on and on. From this 'being in awe' awareness, I became even more enthusiastic about all of life and everything that happens. This heightened awareness literally made me happier with each passing day.

Just recently I looked this word up in the dictionary and realized that one of the definitions means to be inspired by God. Everything in God's great universe is cause for awe and wonder. This is what my own revelation was telling me. To be enthusiastic about everyone and everything allows us to soar and helps us to achieve all we are capable of becoming. Most people look for someone else or something else to inspire them, but enthusiasm and inspiration actually come from within. Everything is within and we have to change our understanding and begin to see that we create our own happiness, enthusiasm, and inspiration. No one else can do it for us.

When we are enthusiastic it draws to us the circumstances and people in life that are also inspiring and enthusiastic. Like attracts like. And although these are the people we would naturally gravitate to and look up to, we can never achieve their state by osmosis. Others can encourage us to see life in an enthusiastic way, but until we actually step into this way of thinking for ourselves, we will never truly know what it's like.

Draw from the wellspring of enthusiasm in your heart. Bring forth this divine nugget which is your birthright and live in the infinite wonder of all the treasures this life has to offer. Welcome each morning with an enthusiastic smile and let that enthusiasm encompass your day. Never think you are alone, unsupported, or defeated. Go to work with a sense of wonder in what this day will bring. How will I be able to help others today? Who is waiting to talk to me? How many projects will I be able to assist in? What wonderful circumstance will I learn from today? Look at everything with the innocence and enthusiasm of a child. Your life will become magical and filled with wonder.

Inspiration Exercises

❤ Think about one incident in your life that you are enthusiastic about, maybe fishing and making lures or perhaps you love tennis, or designing clothes. What are the feelings you get from doing something you like to do? Now write down five rather ordinary chores such as washing the clothes. Can you take this activity and begin to see what divine qualities it would have to make you enthusiastic? Like the refreshing feeling you get at night when you go to bed and snuggle into clean sheets, or put on fresh clean clothes, or even the smell of the detergent or fabric softener. Open up your heart to the enthusiasm that dwells within your own being. How fortunate you are to even have a washing machine or access to one. "What fun. I now get to put a load of clothes in the washing machine." Write out the ways in which you can be enthusiastic about the chores you chose. Now do them with the awareness you just wrote about.

❤ 1. Observe this week those around you who are enthusiastic and those who are unenthusiastic. When you go home in the evening take some time to reflect on these people. What do you think makes someone enthusiastic? How did they get that way? They weren't necessarily born with that trait. Why do you like to be around them? What does it feel like to be in their presence? What makes some people who seem to have challenge after challenge in their life keep on smiling when others are moaning and complaining? Ask a person whose enthusiasm you admire, what makes them that way. They may not even know they are being enthusiastic.

❤ 2. How can you become more enthusiastic, more inspired in your life? Write down the traits that come to your mind and then begin to deliberately practice those qualities. Put them on sticky notes so that as you see them during the day you are reminded to live in the state of enthusiasm. Remember you too can be inspired by just about anything, so practice.

♥ Life is a celebration, an enthusiastic celebration. Today celebrate your life with enthusiasm in all activities. When you get up, think, "How can I help others today? What incredible events will unfold for me today?" Stay in the state that all is well in the world regardless of what is happening to you or around you. At the end of the day reflect on how your day went with this awareness and enthusiastic outlook. Keep practicing this.

CHAPTER 13

Does Your Heart Give Blessings?

Without a doubt, one of the easiest and most joyous gifts to give in this world is blessings. Blessings are free; it feels good to give them, and it makes your life so much richer. It also makes your life so much lighter. First let me explain this lighter part.

There are times, often many times, during the day when little things or big things come up that are not so uplifting or easy to deal with. When this happens just stop and either mentally or out loud say, "I offer my love and blessings to this situation." There is so much power in your thoughts and words it is often hard to fathom. In the chapter *Do You Speak From Your Heart*, I talk about how all words carry energy and whatever you say literally hits the universe and is recorded on the skeins of time. Well it is the same with your thoughts. So whenever you send love and blessings, even mentally, those vibrations are actually going forward and reaching the person and the situation as you speak. There is no time barrier. When you offer love and blessings it happens immediately and it surrounds the situation with a much higher vibration than anger, fear, or frustration. It also pulls you back into your center and helps you deal with the situation in a higher and lighter manner.

Here are some examples of what I am speaking about. Someone calls you on the phone and says, "Nancy, can you come over right away? I just twisted my knee, I can't walk and I need some help." Just say out loud, "I offer you my love and blessings. I'll be right over." You have literally just surrounded your friend in a cocoon of love. Just saying this statement automatically affects another person profoundly and undoubtedly they will say thank you and gratitude will fill their heart even if all they can think about at that moment is the pain they are in.

Your daughter comes home from school in tears and you find out that her boyfriend just jilted her. You can immediately mentally offer her love and blessings and then deal with the crisis.

You're stopped at a light and you see someone in a wheel chair crossing the street, you can once again offer love and blessings.

You're watching the news and an earthquake just happened somewhere; offer love and blessings. Take every opportunity that crosses your awareness to offer this great gift to others. The more you practice the more natural it becomes and pretty soon you find yourself doing it automatically. It becomes a natural behavior of the heart. And on top of that, the more you give these blessings the more they come back to you. What you give, so shall you receive.

Are you beginning to understand what kind of affect you will be having on yourself and others? This act takes but a split second. Think what this world would be like if everyone were on that same wavelength. All it takes is one person to start.

Now here is an idea to take it even a step further. Do you realize that you have the power and ability to program yourself to offer love and blessings to everything all day long? This is the absolute truth. Up until a few years ago I thought that only true saints had this ability. Then I was told directly by a great being that I too had this ability to bless everyone and everything all the time. I understood it intellectually but wasn't able to imbibe the teaching fully, nor was I quite sure how to do it.

As usual, I began to contemplate this principle and came to the conclusion through the back door way of thinking, "Why shouldn't I have this ability?" The great beings have always told us that we are divine, so why not share this divine gift of offering blessings. Besides it couldn't hurt anything and it would feel good. The next step was deciding how I could do it. I decided my eyes were the key. From that day forward to this very day, every morning when I offer my day to God I affirm, "Wherever my eyes light, whatever my eyes see today, no matter how far away it is, even if it is only the shape of a tree two miles away, that absolutely every leaf on that tree is blessed and bathed in love, that everything within my vision receives my blessings and love." It is as simple as that. If you make a habit of doing this or saying your own version every day I assure you that it will become so natural you will wonder why you had never done it before. The mind cannot do anything unless it first becomes a thought. So if you think it is so, it is so.

I can't imagine my life without this practice. I live and breathe this practice to the point where I feel as though I am a walking-talking form of giving love and blessings to everyone and everything all the time. It feels so good and so right to be able to have this understanding and the ability to offer it. It's what we are all about. One of the great benefits is that if I do start to get upset with someone during the day, I almost immediately start to laugh inside because I know my eyes are programmed to give blessings to that person no matter what, so what am I so upset about? They're getting blessings even if I am mad at them. I love it. Think on that one! So give blessings. Let them flow out of you like water over a dam. It will change your perception of yourself and help you begin to see just how powerful you are, not to mention how blessed others and everything will be through your intention.

Give blessings. Give blessings. Give blessings.

Inspiration Exercises

- I do not recommend reading the local newspaper or watching the nightly news, but it will help you to practice offering blessings. So for two or three evenings with every situation you watch or read about, whether it is good or negative say, "I offer my love and blessings to that situation," and any other uplifting blessings you may feel. It is good to offer blessings to uplifting situations too. Your love and joy just makes it more so.

- To help get you in the habit of offering blessings, get out that sweet little invention known as post-it notes, and write it down: Love and Blessings. Put them on the dashboard of your car, on your refrigerator, by your telephone, next to where you sit to watch television. Start giving blessings today and see how good it feels. It will change your perception of yourself and help you begin to see just how powerful you are, and how blessed others and everything will be through your intentions.

- Go for a walk and as you observe all that is around you keep offering your love and blessings to whatever is in front of you and as far as the eye can see.

- Designate at least one hour every day that you mentally offer love and blessing to every person you encounter before beginning to speak to him or her. This will eventually become a natural habit all day long.

CHAPTER 14

Does Your Heart Take Care of Others?

Our purpose on this earth is to serve humankind even on the subtlest of levels. I can think of many stories that demonstrate this, but one that I feel that says it best is found in a book titled, *Why People Don't Heal And How They Can*, by Caroline Myss, Ph.D. This story was shared by a lady taking one of Caroline's workshops and showed exactly how powerful our thoughts and intentions are, especially when we drop into our heart. I will summarize it for you.

This particular woman was so seriously injured in a car accident that she went into an out-of-body experience and was floating above the scene of the accident. She was all of a sudden able to see and hear the reactions from the people that were stuck behind the crash. She could see that some were deeply shaken by what they had witnessed while others were upset that they were being delayed, and this was not what they wanted or felt they needed. From the fifth car behind hers she saw a beautiful swirl of light rising up into the air and then it went down into her own body. She wondered what was happening, and as instantly as she had the thought she was sitting next to that person in her car, who was offering her a prayer. Because of the broadened awareness of the state she was in, she was able to see the license plate and made a mental note of it. She fully recovered from this accident and took it upon herself to track this woman down who had prayed for her. She showed up at her doorstep to offer this woman a bouquet of flowers to say thank you.

I bet that if we could talk to this lady who sent the prayer of blessings, she would be a person who lives in the state of taking care of others very naturally, not even thinking twice about it. This incident shows that our thoughts are as powerful as our actions. This lady's heart was taking care of someone she didn't even know or see. Her mere intention of offering blessings was sent and received from heart to heart instantaneously. No time or space is needed to connect with another in your heart.

I find this incident extremely significant because we are told over and over again that our thoughts are real, that they do go out into the universe in a ripple effect, and what we send out will be returned to us, but very seldom do we have such blatant proof. I urge you to commit this narrative to memory. Every thought you think about someone, whether good or bad, is what you receive back. Does this put a different light on the thoughts you think about others?

There are many ways we can take care of others. There are those who give from their heart out of purity with no strings attached, and then there are those who have so many strings attached that you can almost see them. Where there are strings attached, the giving is not pure. It is not from the heart but from the mind - if I give to you, then in the future I expect something in return. This is akin to buying love or favors. We've all experienced it and we've all done it. There is often a payoff in being nice. But the pure heart, the sweet heart, the heart that gives for the sake of giving is the highest.

Does Your Heart Take Care of Others?

I love that bumper sticker that reads, "I stop to perform random acts of kindness." Just be good to others and be good to others just because. Take care of others for the sheer joy of it. Even if you can't physically help another, your heart can take care of another through its intentions. Wish well to others. Life is too short not to.

Inspiration Exercises

- ♥ Random Acts of Kindness: Today as you go about your chores and work become aware of little acts of kindness you can do for others without any reward or payoff expected in return. How many can your heart see to do today? Act on them. Don't count them - just do them. Let your day be filled with divine energy and the willingness to allow the love in your heart to help everyone you can. If you are in a situation where you think you are not able to help others like in a hospital bed, where others are helping you, just remember you <u>are</u> helping them by making their day brighter and lighter, even if it is only to appreciate them and compliment them on some little thing that they are doing well. It is an act of kindness to come from your heart and express your love in a simple "Thank you for always being so gentle when you draw my blood," or "Thank you for explaining this procedure to me. It helps take away my fear of having to go through it," or "Thank you for always coming as soon as you can when I call for help." Then silently from your heart offer them blessings and love.

- ♥ Today do at least two random acts of kindness for yourself. What a grand concept. Do something sweet for yourself that would be uplifting and healthy that you may not usually do. An example may be to give your body a walk or allow yourself to read an uplifting book to fill your mind with wisdom and understanding to help you grow and expand. This random act of kindness for yourself does have a payoff, a very positive one at that, if it meets the criteria of uplifting and healthy.

- ♥ Take ten minutes three different times today, sit quietly and do positive affirmations such as "My body vibrates with health and vitality right now," or "I breathe in love and breathe out blessings." This is a wonderful practice to develop. As unnecessary or negative thoughts start to float through your mind repeat positive affirmations. You begin to program yourself in a different mindset and you begin to have more control over any unwanted thoughts.

CHAPTER 15

Does Your Heart Forgive Others?

When the heart can live in forgiveness it is a jewel indeed. I love the way the word forgive can be divided, love is *forgiving* - love is *for giving*. No matter how you put it, forgiving is love. It is the willingness to pardon, to cancel or remit a debt, to give up your wanting to punish or hurt someone and replacing those negative feelings with the love of forgiveness. It's a willingness to move on with your life and not be consumed by events of the past.

To discuss this topic means we have to look at anger because to forgive, in essence, very often means that you are angry either with yourself or another. To lead a productive and happy life you want to unclutter the negativities of the heart and stop being a victim. This requires forgiveness.

There are many avenues we could take to look at anger, but let's use one that is close to so many peoples' hearts - our families. I work with many people, young and old alike who have issues with their parents. You need to understand that your parents gave you everything they could at any given time. Your parents couldn't give you what they didn't have. Let me repeat this. Your parents could not give you what they did not have. This is so important. If your parents did not give you love or understanding, it is because they did not know what it was like to be truly loved or understood themselves. This goes for any kind of treatment you may have received. We choose our parents for lessons we need to learn. Sometimes we chose the parents we did to learn the greatest of lessons about how not to be. We need to go beyond their limitations and learn to have the qualities they did not possess.

It's so much easier to blame your parents for falling short than it is to forgive them. It does not mean that because you forgive them that you have to be around them. Just thank them for giving what they were able to give, no matter how little it may have been. View your life from a different perspective. For example, if your parents were cruel to you, did you learn how important it was to be compassionate toward people? Did you learn from their lack of compassion? Do you now live in compassion for others, or are you just repeating the patterns of your parents and treating your own children with cruelty because that is the way you were treated? Do you see how you can learn from the shortcomings of others? When you have this perspective your life will take on new meaning.

Families can be the greatest place to practice forgiveness. They can push your buttons in an instant. Usually your spouse or children can continually help to keep you on the practicing edge of forgiving. There can be so many little irritating things that make it difficult to live with someone, such as throwing your coat on the couch instead of hanging it up, or not cleaning up the kitchen when you're done cooking, or putting the toilet paper roll on the spindle in the wrong direction. There will always be challenges, whether in your own family or in the world, but how you deal with these circumstances will be determined by your ability to remain centered in your heart and the strength of your heart in forgiving.

When we are upset or angry with another we have this tendency to replay the incident in our minds over and over again about how some injustice was done to us. It is often easier to wallow in victimhood than to forgive. Getting angry is an addiction. Anger can and will consume you and make you a bitter person. It can also cause illness and disease.

To be able to forgive someone, your heart must be very beautiful. To not offer back cruelty or insults takes an even stronger heart. When you forgive you show the greatness of your soul.

Here are some tips in dealing with anger:

First of all, it is important to not stuff your anger inside yourself, but at the same time it does not mean to live and wallow in it day in and day out making everyone else suffer who has to listen to you vent, telling everyone how you feel and what wrongs have been committed against you. You do live in your body, and you do have feelings that cannot be ignored. It is important to acknowledge how you feel and get to the root of the anger, but you need to move on. You cannot stay in the space of anger or it will destroy you over time. One little anger on top of another little anger, builds up until you explode or turn out to be a very bitter and overall unhappy and angry person. We all know people who live in this state. They do not forgive, period.

One thing you can do is to address each issue right away or as soon as appropriate and offer feedback to the person you feel an emotional charge toward. Often expressing the way you feel in a caring way can transform an experience. If another person is not willing to understand you then your feelings may be leading you to leave a situation that is not for your highest good.

Another way to address an issue is to write it down. Write your story and your feelings. I know some people who have a notebook just for frustrations. If you need to vent, do it on paper. Just try it. You will be surprised at the beneficial outcome of this process. Then offer your anger to God. Note, I said offer it. Do not be angry with God, don't throw it at God or it will be thrown back, but offer it to God with all your heart to lift your heart to the pure space of forgiveness. If you feel you can't love someone then ask God to love them through you.

Take every situation, learn from it, and let unconditional forgiveness flow from your heart. Don't hold on to old memories, hurts, or grudges. Remember love is forgiving, *for giving.* When forgiveness is complete, you will feel serene, kind, happy, and loved. Your life will reflect your forgiving nature and you will not be overwhelmed in your own anguish. You will be filled with compassion and attract love and joy into your life.

Inspiration Exercises

- ♥ Almost everyone has someone or a situation they are carrying anger about. I invite you to examine a situation that may be bothering you and has been repeating itself over and over in your head. Examine this experience and try to take it to the root cause. Can you see what truly caused the anger and can you offer your love to it so you can move on? Even if you can't feel forgiveness toward that person or situation every time you think of it say, "I offer my love and blessings to so and so or to this situation." Sit quietly and ask God what the lesson is to be learned from this challenge so you can move forward and not repeat the same pattern that caused this situation to occur.

  Each time you offer love and blessings to a situation you are wrapped up in; it develops an increasing awareness on a subtle level of forgiveness. Eventually you will begin to be able to feel the situation diminish itself in your mind and you will find yourself thinking about it less and less. The anger will begin to dissolve and dissipate under its own weight. This sometimes takes a long time, but be patient with yourself and keep doing it. It will work.

- ♥ To children of parents who did not have a good experience growing up: Sit quietly and begin to reflect on the characteristics of your parents and how you were treated or not treated. Can you go back in time in your mind or do research on their backgrounds to see how they may have been raised? For the most part you will usually find that if you were an unwanted child at least one of your parents was also an unwanted child, or if you were beaten or emotionally abused by your parents they too may have been beaten or abused as a child and so they grew up thinking this was the norm. More importantly, have you patterned yourself after them? Now looking from the premise that you actually chose them as parents before you took a body, what are the lessons you need to learn from them? How have they helped you learn to be or not to be? If you are stuck in the feeling that they hindered you, how can you move past this and step into your own beauty and compassion for them and others?

There comes a point in your life during your young adult years that you become aware, even if unconsciously, that you have a choice to make in this world on how to be. You learn that you now have control over your own circumstances and you can begin to decide, subtly or not so subtly, what you want to be like and who you want to be like. If you are not happy with yourself or circumstances you have created you can now make a conscious choice to change. Step into love and forgive your parents and move on. Remember, love is *forgiving* and also *for giving* to yourself so you can make positive changes in your life.

♥ Make two vertical columns across the top of a piece of paper. In the first column write down the positive traits of each of your parents. In the second column write down your own positive traits. Now leaving space to add more positive qualities as they come to mind, draw a horizontal line across the page under these two columns. Under the first column again, write down the negative traits of each of your parents and then under the second column write down your negative traits. Can you see a correlation? It is wonderful if you have embodied your parents' positive behaviors, but what about the negative tendencies? Lessons were put in front of you so you could grow beyond the limitations of your parents. If you have embodied negative tendencies from them how can you shift these negative tendencies to positive ones? You can do it. Write down your ideas. Begin to shift your awareness into a positive framework and practice uplifting and positive traits. It first takes awareness, then the intent, and then the practice.

CHAPTER 16

Does Your Heart Love the Animals?

Are you aware that animals actually can and do communicate with one another? That they can also communicate with you if you will let them? Now I am not talking about that humble, sad, forlorn, "Oh poor me," or "How on earth could you ever leave me alone?" look you get from your dog as he sees you walk out the door to go to work each day. Nor am I talking about the cat's mournful meow as she gently entwines herself through and around your legs with the look, "How can you not understand that I am absolutely famished right now and you still continue to do what you're doing when I want food?" Yes, these ways of communicating are definitely valid, but animals have more subtle communication skills as well.

Animal lovers of this world know that with a little practice they can actually tune in mentally and hear what the needs of their pets are and how they can best support them. You have the ability to do this too. Animal communicators (people who can actually hear what the animals have to say) when called upon, have made a profound difference in how owners relate to their pets. If you have ever used an animal communicator, you all of a sudden begin to see that there is a lot more happening on on this planet than meets the eye.

I don't want to lose you in my esoteric wisdom of animal communication, but I want to make you aware that in the hierarchy of the animal kingdom, they do have feelings, wants, and needs just like you do. If they are sick they can tell you what is the matter with them, exactly what is the matter with them. They are also here to teach you many lessons if you will let them. Even if you do not realize it, they are still teaching and supporting you.

I have many amazing stories about animal communication so let me share a couple with you. A friend of mine was given two beautiful birds that she loved and took great care of. All of a sudden their behavior changed and the moment she would return home in the evening these birds would start going wild. Instead of greeting her with their joyful chirping they would start screeching and jumping all over the cage as if they were angry and upset about something. My friend couldn't understand this unusual behavior and knew something was drastically wrong as it continued day after day. She finally decided to call an animal communicator she had heard about from a reliable source to see if this mystery could be solved. What happened as a result of this was quite extraordinary. The animal communicator tuned into the birds and they told her that every time their master was leaving the house the lights would begin to go on and off. The birds went on to explain that they associated the light coming on with their master coming home and when she didn't walk through the door they would be filled with anxiety that they were being abandoned. By the time she got home at night the birds were beside themselves and trying to tell her what was happening.

So my friend retraced her steps as she left the next morning to see what would cause these so called lights to go on and off when she wasn't at home. Sure enough she discovered there was a short circuit in her entry alarm system that she would turn on when she left. She solved the problem and the birds immediately went back to being serene and calm.

Here is another story that I feel is very touching. Another friend of mine was living in a mountainous region. It was the middle of winter with lots of snow on the ground and quite late in the evening when she arrived home. A fair distance was before her as she left her car to walk to her house. She was tired, yet in a very peaceful state as she remembers, just drinking in the beauty of the snowflakes as they shimmered from the reflection of the moon. All of a sudden she felt as if someone was watching her. She stopped and there not more than ten feet from her was a huge buck deer standing stock-still and staring at her. She was startled for she knew that these large animals when provoked can be dangerous. As she looked at him the buck looked directly and very distinctly into her eyese and with great mental power said to her, "What is your intention?" My friend was so amazed and dazed she stumbled over her words and said back to him mentally, "I am very tired and I live over there, pointing toward her home, and I cannot get there unless I go by you. I am not here to hurt you. I just want to go to bed." The buck looked at her, blinked his eyes, and made a nodding motion with his head. At that moment a female deer that had been hiding in the shadows came around to the side of the buck and offered her blessings to my friend. There is more to this story, but I am sharing this part of it just to tantalize you in learning more about animals. It was one of the most memorable and sacred events my friend had ever experienced. Up until that time she had never had any communication with animals.

This event appears as if it were one of those windows of opportunities that we hear about every so often, where the veil between worlds is dropped and we can see reality from another perspective. That veil that keeps us separated from all that is, is becoming thinner and thinner with each passing day. I'm sharing these stories with you to help you open the door of your heart to a new dimension of seeing animals from a different point of view.

Hurt not the animals but treat them with the greatest of respect. Love the animals of this earth with all your heart for they exist for many more reasons than to just provide us with enjoyment to observe or to comfort us. We co-exist with one another on this plane to help each other grow. We both very consciously come here for things we chose to offer or to learn from one another. Animals are evolving just as we are and in serving and loving the animals we truly serve and love ourselves.

Inspiration Exercises

- ❤ A wonderful exercise to practice whenever you see any animal is to say, "I offer you blessings of love." This creates an immediate bond between you and the animal. Believe me when I tell you that the animals do receive and feel your blessings. Look for animals, insects, reptiles, birds, and water creatures this week to communicate with. Better yet go to a zoo and do this practice.

- ❤ Every single time you see your pet today say, "I love you and am filled with gratitude you are in my life." This will get you in the habit of saying this to all other animals too.

- ❤ Read a book about animal communication. There are now entire sections in bookstores that deal with this popular topic. It is becoming more and more accepted as main stream that animals can and do talk with humans when humans sincerely make the effort to try and understand them. Even if you may not be interested in developing personal communication systems with animals, by reading even one book about them, you will open up an awareness within you as to their incredible intelligence and amazing abilities.

CHAPTER 17

Do You Let Your Heart Smile?

There is never a moment when your own true heart is not benevolently smiling on you. The heart space in and of itself is absolutely pure. To remain pure depends on what you put in that heart space. With negative thoughts it becomes tainted. The good news is that all we have to do to purify our heart space is to start dropping old wounds, hurts, and negativities, and replace them with love and genuine smiles. We need to offer our benevolent smiles to the rest of the world. A simple genuine smile bridges every language barrier on earth.

There are many kinds of smiles. In another chapter I talked about pasted-on smiles (Either I smile or I get fired). Try some of these on for size. I love you smiles. Smiles of laughter. The snickering, snide, or rude smile. The I-told-you-so smile. The smile of concern. I'm sure you can list others. But the genuine smile, the one that spontaneously comes from the heart; that's the one that softens all the burdens of life and brings joy to all who receive it, and give it.

At the young age of seventeen I was trained to smile. Yes, trained to smile. Not that I didn't smile a lot, because smiling was second nature to me, but I was trained to smile all the time. I decided I wanted to become a professional model and so my parents sent me to modeling school. The training on how to walk, how to present yourself on and off a runway, and how to smile was of immense value to me, especially as the years went by. Smiling becomes a good habit if you give it a chance.

At one point in my life I worked for a large retail company and it was mandatory to smile. It wasn't put quite so bluntly as that though. We were taught that when we walked on the sales floor we needed to drop any of our personal agendas and problems and smile, be there as a sounding board for the customers and their problems - to make them happy and to sell, sell, sell. We learned that no one really cared if you had a fight with your spouse that morning, your child was sick, or if you were going to divorce court that afternoon. We were there to smile and serve.

Well, you know what, there is a lot to be said about that philosophy because not only is it true that others don't want to hear your problems at work, they don't want to hear them away from work either. Everyone has enough of their own problems to deal with in this day and age. After listening to customers all day long you actually begin to count your blessings because it usually turns out that you are more fortunate than they. To be able to drop your own agenda and to only concentrate on helping others is one of the best ways to forget about your own troubles. A great saint once said to stop crying and feeling sorry for yourself, put on a smile and go help someone else who is less fortunate than you.

If your smile comes from a place of love, it is beneficial to all who observe it. We just need to do it a lot more often. More than once in my life I have been described as a person who smiles a lot. I like to smile. It not only makes me feel good but it makes others feel good too. Life is so much easier if taken with a smile. It makes you happier and healthier. It is a proven fact that if you are a person who can smile at life you will live longer, be happier, and people will seek your company.

It doesn't take much practice to learn to smile a lot. It's just something you do. I bet you have known people who never cracked a smile. These are very serious people. Just how happy do you think they are? Do you want to spend time around them? I don't think so. Practice smiling. I have diffused many situations in my life by just smiling from my heart.

I remember one time when I was living in India I had to catch one of the local trains. Now this can be an experience in and of itself that I could write a book about. I fought for space just to get on the train. Now if you could get fifty into one of these train cars it would be crowded, but try two hundred! Packed to the hilt. Eventually the further out of the city you go, a tiny bit more space becomes available as people get off. After standing like a packed sardine for forty minutes I finally was able to wedge my way to a seat. I was so tired that I closed my eyes to rest for about five minutes. I was silently sitting there when all of a sudden I felt an incredible wave of energy coming at me. When I opened my eyes I had no less than sixty people just staring at me. Staring is a very common trait in this country, which by now I was used to. Being tall and blonde did make me a bit unusual, but to have all theses solemn eyes focused on me at once as if I was going to give a great speech was shocking. I took one giant glance at everyone and then gave one big giant smile and acknowledged every one of them. In that instant every one of them smiled back at the same time. I hadn't said a word. It was one of the sweetest moments I recall while being in the city. They couldn't speak a word of English and I couldn't speak a word of Hindi, but that one universal smile from each of us left us all glowing.

You can make almost anyone smile if you are genuine. One practice I like to do is to smile at all kinds of people when I'm in my car. People who look the most serious or have an attitude are the ones I like to get to smile. Like if I am just waiting to pull out of my driveway and another resident pulls in, I may not even know them but I smile at them. They can have the most serious look on their face but nine times out of ten they will smile back. It's like welcoming them home. Every time I let a jogger have the right of way I smile at them and think good thoughts for their safety, and for the most part they usually smile and give a quick wave of thank you. The key in both these instances is to be genuine and let it be a smile from the heart. A smile shows that you care about another human being along the path of life.

I have literally worked with people from all over this globe where neither of us could speak the others' language. A heartfelt smile is often all I have needed to communicate to the other person, "I love you, I understand, and I want to help you." A person can feel so loved through a smile, so be free with them. Offer your genuine smiles of love and compassion everywhere. Let smiles shape your day and your destiny.

Inspiration Exercises

- ♥ For one hour each day this week concentrate on smiling at everyone. Smile from the heart space and point of genuineness. If you are a person who is not used to smiling, others may question your intentions such as, "What is he or she up to?" Who cares! After the week is over begin practicing this technique for an hour in the morning and then for one hour in the evening even if you are just at home. As you chop vegetables for a salad smile at them for the sustenance they offer you. Smile at your computer that allows you be connected to the world so easily. Smile at your bathtub that gives you relaxation, and smile at your bed that allows you to get a good night's rest. Practice, practice, practice and don't 'just' smile; let it come from a heart filled with gratitude.

- ♥ Observe smiles today and see how many kinds you can identify like with those I described in this chapter. Begin to see the difference in the myriad of smiles that come your way and to others. Especially look for the genuine smiles and how they affect you or someone else. Become aware of how smiling affects those around you. Is your boss smiling today or is it a 'Stay away from her office day'? How does your boss's smile affect you - your heart? How does it set your day? Begin to understand how important a smile can be to others.

- ♥ When you are out in public walking down the street or in the park, with everyone you encounter YOU be the first to smile at another as someone approaches you. I have walked the streets of New York many times and you will hear almost everyone say that New Yorkers never smile, don't look at you as they pass, or are rude, etc. I have found this to be just the opposite. As you pass someone there is almost always a point where they will look up at you if only for a split second. Have your smile on ready to say hello. Yes, I may have smiled first, but I almost always got a smile back and often a friendly comment. Yes, I may have had to be the one to step forward, but because I did others were given the opportunity to let their heart smile too. It will work for you too, but even if by chance it doesn't, then you have lost nothing. You can just send them love. Don't feel the other person has to smile first. I tried it everywhere in Manhattan - on the bus, in the subway, on the streets, and in stores. Open your heart. Let sunshine in. Be happy. Smile. You have the opportunity to lighten this world through your smiles.

CHAPTER 18

Do You Follow Your Heart?

How many of you can say without a doubt you are following your greatest heart's desire? And what does that really mean? There are very few people in the world today who can say they like their jobs or that they are happy with their life. So many people feel stuck, unable to move forward into their true hearts' desires. Why is this? What is keeping you from doing what you want in life?

The usual answers are: I don't have enough money to do what I want, it's too hard to start over, or it would require a change in my life style or my family's life style if I did what I wanted to do. Think about this. How much do you really want it, and wouldn't your family want you to be happy? I also hear, "I know I want to do something else in my life but I'm not sure what." These are all excuses so you can complain about how unhappy and unfulfilled you are. There are *always* solutions to being able to satisfy your heart's desires, but maybe no one has ever shown you how.

Many years ago when I was on a ferryboat shuttle I happened to sit next to a woman who struck up a conversation with me. We both just happened to be taking the shuttle to the same class! She was telling me about her life's work and was so enthusiastic about what she did that I want to share with you how she followed her heart.

She explained to me that she read this book one day called *Wishcraft* by Barbara Sher. This is a book that teaches you how to find the work you love and how to go about getting there. She followed the exercises in the book and immediately knew she wanted to do what the author of this book did. She lived in Seattle and found that this author lived in New York. She had very little money and could not afford to take this author's classes to learn how to do this type of work for a profession, but on a gamble, she bought a plane ticket to New York and showed up on this author's doorstep one day and said, "Hello, I'm so and so and I want to learn how to do what you do. I want to help others follow their heart and to be able to help them succeed at what they want to do in this life. I don't have the money to take your classes but I am willing to be your apprentice. Will you let me apprentice under you?" The author said yes and the rest is history.

I had never heard of this book before, although it was written many years ago. It sounded interesting but I knew what I wanted to do in my life and I was actively working at the process of achieving my life's goal at the time so I never read the book. I did, however, check it out the next time I was at the local bookstore; and I too thought it was so inspiring that I began recommending this book to others who were struggling with their hearts' desires and how to achieve them. It has helped many friends and acquaintances over the years.

What I am getting at in this story is that this person followed her inner longing and was doing what made her heart sing. She may have taken action a little differently than the average person would have, but she knew what she wanted and went for it. When we do what we love our whole world changes. Even if we can only partially do what we want, something is better than nothing. For example, you may be a person who would love to give up your 8 to 5 job and run a greenhouse. There are so many options just in this one scenario alone. You could start planning on how you will accomplish this goal and work towards it, or if you feel this is not appropriate for you at this time in your life, then do something along the same lines that will give you the joy of this type of work. It will satisfy your deep longing and bring you happiness. If you couldn't quit your job perhaps you could get one of those backyard greenhouses and do your gardening there. If you don't have a yard you could create a little nook in your home dedicated only to plants or put up a bookshelf where you keep only gardening books. Use your imagination. The possibilities are endless. The point is to do something about it. Even following your heart on a small scale can bring great rewards.

For years I wanted to know God. I would read all kinds of books about great beings and would pray for a master. Then when I found the spiritual path that totally resonated with my entire being I knew that I wanted the experience of living part of my life in an ashram (monastery) with my meditation teacher. I still had two children at home and knew my responsibilities were to finish raising them with great love. When they were safely on their own, I could then follow my heart's desire. Since I couldn't just up and leave home at the time, I made my home my ashram. I set up my altar and started to do spiritual practices of meditating and chanting and continued to read holy books. I slowly began to unburden my life by letting go of material things. The time came when my children had established themselves on their own so I sold everything I had left. (I had originally started with a two-story house, a full basement and five bedrooms, all of which were completely furnished.) It took almost eight years to reach my goal of going to live with my meditation teacher but in the meantime by creating my own sacred space and living as if I were already in the ashram I was able to keep my enthusiasm up for what my heart desired. For the next five years I lived between India and New York ashrams doing exactly what my heart wanted to do. It was the most sublime and profound, yet challenging, experience of my life.

When I moved out of the ashram I started an exciting new and different life. I literally felt like a twenty year old just stepping out on my own for the first time. It has been an exhilarating experience. If I can do this, so can you. You and I are no different from one another. It just takes a desire, a longing and some planning. It can never materialize if it is not a thought first. Once it is a thought, develop it and work with it. Your visions of today are the accomplishments of your tomorrow.

I have to offer you this one last delightful story because it summarizes the fact that it does not matter how old you are to follow your dream. Just recently I was invited to go to this class to learn some tips about publishing a book. I thought it sounded interesting and so I went. It turned out to be an ongoing class about how to write a book. There were about fifteen people ranging in age from about thirty to eighty. I sat next to the sweetest, very old woman and we shared some of the handouts. She was frail of body and needed to use both hands to write due to her arthritis and yet here she was at her age enthusiastically writing her story. There were others just like her, all with their own story and determined to accomplish one of their hearts' desires. I think of this class often and send them blessings on accomplishing what they have always wanted to do. It was a wonderful sight to behold.

There have been too many success stories to believe you can't do what you really want to do in this life. This universe is abundant. Know that if you have desires that will make your heart soar there is some way just waiting to be found so that you can do what it is you love in this world. So, what does your heart want to do that it

Do You Follow Your Heart?

is not doing? If you do not know or want to get started in making your heart sing, do the following exercises.

Inspiration Exercises

- ❤ If you know what you would like to do, then take a block of time today and reflect on how you can go about doing those things that would help you live in joy. Write them down. Forget any obstacles that may come across your mind to prevent you from your desires. How would it look if you could do it full time, part time, or simply as a hobby? Maybe doing it as a hobby would be the first step to see if you really want to do this full time. How could you start? What would be your first step? Perhaps doing research on it, or it may be something you would have to purchase. Ask others what ideas they may have to help you or inspire you. You will be surprised at the inspiration and creative ideas others can offer. Develop a plan on how to achieve it step by step. Then take the first step towards your goal. Perhaps this may mean to purchase a book on your special topic, take a class, write out a financial plan on how to begin to accomplish it, or clearing a space in your home to make ready for it. Your intention is everything. Take the steps, ask for guidance from spirit, and you will be surprised at how the universe will support you.

- ❤ If you are unhappy with your job or activities and don't have a clue as to what you can or want to do, purchase *Wishcraft* by Barbara Sher. You can begin right now by starting to write down twenty enjoyable things you most like to do then taking each item and looking at how often you actually do each one, and how often you would like to do each activity. You will begin to get a picture of what makes your heart happy, and how balanced or imbalanced these enjoyable activities actually are given precedence in your life. It can also be the first concrete step in beginning to incorporate things you love into your life. *Wishcraft* is a delightful book on how to incorporate what you love to do in your work or just developing and putting in place what you love to do into your lifestyle. There are also many other good books that have been written that can help you set the wheels in motion to find your perfect job. Go to the bookstore or library and do some research. This will get you motivated and will be the first step you can actively take to making your dreams a reality. The first step will lead to the second and then the third and so on.

CHAPTER 19

Do You Let Your Heart Meditate?

Meditation has become a common American buzzword. It is the "in" thing to do if you are anybody. Let us take a look at the deeper meaning of what meditation really is and why is it so beneficial to us. This practice of going within is an incredible and powerful process. Some people meditate because their doctor told them it would help them to lower their blood pressure or to help them with controlling their stress level. If you are one of these meditators, let me tell you, there is much more going on than just this, much more than you can imagine. It doesn't matter for what purpose you meditate. When you meditate you receive the greatest of gifts your heart has to offer.

Meditation is that state of awareness which results when one becomes absorbed in the Self. Through meditation we experience the peace, courage, love, and strength that spring from contact with our divine essence. Over time this inner contact begins to infuse our experience of daily life, freeing us from anxiety, anger, and fear and filling our days with joy.

In meditation you take a journey inward from your physical body and the state of waking consciousness to deeper levels of your being and subtler states of consciousness until at last you enter into union with your own true Self and the entire universe.

Whether you realize it or not, all day long you actually meditate - on things outside yourself. These are the thoughts of the mind. Whatever you think about is what you are meditating on, or focusing on. Focus your mind on a movie you have seen; the mind plays the movie a thousand times. Focus your mind on your friend; it brings about great love. Focus your mind on your enemy; it fills your mind with hatred. Wherever you focus your mind, the mind has the ability to absorb it like a dry sponge.

When you meditate, your goal is to let the mind rest and not think thoughts at all. This, as many of you well know, is easier said than done. Just try thinking of absolutely nothing for one minute. Maybe try thirty seconds. Good luck! This is one of the main reasons you sleep at night, which is its own form of meditation. We turn within to renew and rejuvenate the body. When you go to bed at night and your mind is thinking and thinking, making plans and worrying, it is difficult to go to sleep. There comes a point at which, for a split second, you have no thoughts at all and you fall into slumber.

In the same way when you practice meditation, there is a fraction of a moment when your mind stops, and in that moment you fall into meditation. Through practice you increase the duration of this moment of one-pointedness.

When your thoughts become fewer and fewer, your body becomes healthier and you are able to enjoy your life more. As you enjoy your life more and more, you are able to experience higher and higher realities within your own human system. At this point you can truly serve humanity and the world around you in ways beyond your own comprehension.

Some people have the idea that if you meditate you become brainless. It is actually the opposite. To be able to meditate requires a high standard of intelligence. When you become firmly absorbed in the practice, the intellect is purified, and then the intellect can perceive the Truth.

I warmly invite you to experience the practice of meditation. If you can make this a daily routine, even if you have only ten minutes each day, you will begin to experience the benefits that this practice brings, not only more peace in your life, but a greater sense of the divine.

Allow yourself to go inside to the space of the heart and let yourself become absorbed in its light. As Bhagawan Nityananda, a great saint, once said, "The heart is the hub of all sacred places. Go there and roam." Or as Jesus said, "The kingdom of heaven lies within."

Inspiration Exercises

- ♥ As with anything, the more you practice the more it becomes a habit. To aid in developing this beautiful practice I suggest you designate a special place where it is quiet, comfortable and peaceful. Try to meditate at the same time every day and for a set amount of time. Increase the time frame gradually up to an hour when you can. Even if you only have ten minutes a day it is better than nothing at all. Also the practice of sitting on a woolen blanket helps to hold in the meditation energy as you meditate in the same spot every day. This makes dropping into meditation easier over time.

Meditation Instructions:

- ◆ Sit in a comfortable upright posture whether on a chair or cross-legged on the floor. Keep your spine straight but not rigid. Close your eyes. Place your hands comfortably in your lap or place your hands on your knees with thumb and forefinger touching.

- ◆ Relax your entire body, noticing where you may have tension and consciously releasing it.

- ◆ Begin to become aware of your breathing. As you breathe in and out very deliberately, watch the breath, allowing the rhythm of the breath to pull your focus inside. Breathe in deep and breathe out long for four or five breaths.

- Now begin to breathe naturally. If thoughts come up, let them go. Keep bringing your attention back to the breath, watching it flow in and out.

- When you are finished, bring yourself slowly out of meditation to honor what has taken place. Even if you had a challenge trying to release thoughts and your mind remained busy, your intention alone allows you to meditate whether you realize it or not.

- Keep practicing for the rest of your life and increase the amount of time you spend meditating. It is often recommended that an hour is sufficient, but again, even if you only have ten minutes, at least commit to that.

- ♥ Visit a spiritual bookstore and explore their meditation book section. My favorite book on this topic is *Meditate* by Swami Muktananda, which can be ordered if it is not carried at the store. There are many other books and tapes that offer other meditation tips and techniques.

CHAPTER 20

Do You Live From Your Heart?

When it is all said and done will you be able to say you lived in your heart in this lifetime? Were you good to <u>everyone</u>? Did you give your best to this world? Did you love unconditionally? Did you listen to others with all you heart? Did you offer your thoughts to seeing the best in everyone? Did you wish everyone well? Did you welcome each person that came into your life with love? Did you always speak highly of everyone? Did the words that you spoke reflect the heart's compassion and understanding?

These are high and lofty goals and we can actually achieve them. I'm positive that no one could give a whole hearted "Yes" to each one of these questions, yet that is how you should be dealing with the world and with one another all the time. The fortunate thing is that every single minute is a new beginning. God does not care how many times you think you fail at not doing, or getting, something right. The point is that you try and keep trying. There is absolutely no such thing as a mistake. Of this I am positive. This world is a test and is set up to continually register your responses and how you react to see where you are in the space of living in and from your heart. So look at these tests as a big game to play and keep trying to be a loftier human being with each passing day. The point is to just keep trying.

Let your practice of learning to be in the heart be joyful and light. As you do, so you become. This is not a pass or fail test. Keep practicing. Remember your opportunities are endless to start anew. Pretty soon your practice becomes habit just like anything else. And once this good habit is established, you begin to see your life take on new meaning and dimension.

To live in your heart is the highest, for once you have established that connection you'll find that everyone wants to be around you. Everyone seeks your advice because you have aligned yourself with the highest principles of life, to see the greatest in others and to speak with love, compassion, understanding, and wisdom.

Inspiration Exercises

♥ Take any one of the questions listed in the first paragraph of this chapter, write it down and keep it with you during the day where you can see it. Start keeping a journal with a different question at the top of each page so you can go back and review to see progress you have made over time. After choosing your question of the day keep referring back to it, keeping the question on paper with you where you can view it often and look at the number of times you had the opportunity to come from your heart with the question you chose.

Example: "Am I listening to others with all my heart today?" Were you actually able to listen to others intently with your whole heart and soul, only there for *them* as they were trying to relay to you something that was troubling them; or were you doing something else at the same time, like watching television or thumbing through a magazine?

Example: "Am I giving my best to the world every minute today?" Did you give your best or did you go through the day half-heartedly? How many times during the day did you do a task just because you had to, not giving yourself to it fully?

Be aware today just how often you did or didn't live from your heart. Become your own best observer. Tonight before retiring, review your day and journal the incidences, your responses, and observations of your behavior for the question you chose to work with. Give yourself good feedback for every time you consciously came from your heart. Every day choose a different question to practice this trait of living from the heart. Fill a whole journal with this information. Every so often go through your journal as you progress and see how you have subtly changed. You will be amazed.

♥ Before you go to bed at night take a few minutes to review your day and look at the times you made the conscious decision to act from your heart. How many times did you act from your heart naturally and how many times did it take an awareness of your intention to come from your heart space? Where could you have improved and how? As you keep working with the questions in this chapter you will begin to make yourself continually aware of dropping into the heart when dealing with everyone.

CHAPTER 21

Do You Speak From Your Heart?

Walking takes an amazing amount of energy. Just try not talking for one day and see how energized you feel. Most esoteric philosophies encourage people to keep silent for periods of time. Notice the silence of a church, a sanctuary, an ashram, or a monastery. These sacred places are silent so you can go inside, connect with your heart, and listen to what your heart has to share with you. Times of silence replenish your body, mind, and heart. Silence can heal on many levels.

That's why, when you do speak, it is important to do so from the heart. Heartfelt communication occurs when you follow the **Four Golden Rules of Speech:**

    Is it true?
    Is it necessary?
    Is it kind and uplifting?
    Is it the right time?

If everyone were to practice these golden nuggets of speech, peace and joy would permeate our interactions.

Is what you are saying true? Before it rolls off your tongue, make sure you have your facts straight. So many rumors get started from incorrect information. Just recently, an acquaintance told me something about a good friend of mine that didn't sound at all in character. I stated very clearly at the time that the scenario did not ring true. When I next saw my good friend and asked her about what I heard, she was dumbfounded. None of it had happened at all. She then went about setting the record straight, contacting the people who might have heard the erroneous story. The misinformation not only wasted my time and her time, but the time of many others. How often has this happened to you? Remember to check and double check if the information you are sharing is true, or if it even needs to be shared.

How much of what you say is totally unnecessary? Truly speaking, probably most of it is. The goal here is to keep the unnecessary to a minimum. Too much superfluous talk actually impedes real communication. You probably know someone who babbles on and on. Often times, what they are saying is not only unnecessary but also gossip to boot. They talk just to talk while you become exhausted just listening to them. Even if their prattle goes in one ear and out the other, it still uses up your energy to process it.

Then there are people who just can't wait to be the bearer of bad news. This becomes such a habit for them, they do not even realize they are doing it. The courageous and most loving way to respond in this situation is to compassionately confront the person with something like, "Do you have any good news you would like to share with me? I feel uncomfortable in our conversations when I continually hear about the misfortunes of others." If you cannot do this, then the next best thing is to excuse yourself politely and walk away. It is best to maintain a distance with anyone that surrounds your heart in negativity. Often times we speak inappropriately, adding to gossip or negativity, because we just want to keep the connection open with another person. We just want contact. We want relationship. Yet, sometimes saying nothing at all is the kindest and most loving act you can offer to another human being. You can say it all by just sitting with someone, just being together in the silence of the heart.

Is your speech kind and uplifting? The old adage still holds true: If you can't say something nice to or about someone then don't say anything at all. We love to be around people who exhibit kindness and love in their speech. When you hear someone speak highly and with honor about others, you feel that person would say the same about you. You feel safe with them, as if they are your ally.

Is it the right time? Some times are much better than others for delivering information, especially if it is unpleasant. If you need to convey disheartening information, try, if possible, to give it in the morning or early afternoon. This gives the person time for reflection and processing. News in the evening affords little time for resolution and causes a restless or sleepless night.

If you practice these golden nuggets of speech and make them a habit, you will find it only takes a second to decide if you should or shouldn't say something. If you make the highest effort to plant only seeds of love, you will find your life abundantly joyous. You always have a choice in what you offer to the universe - and what it returns to you.

Inspiration Exercises

- ♥ Commit the **Four Golden Rules of Speech** to your mind and heart. Put them on notecards at work, home, and in the car. Memorize them so they become etched in the recesses of your consciousness. Repeat them outloud first thing in the morning, before entering your work place, at lunch, before meetings or before coming home in the evening. This will get you in the habit of thinking about what is going to come out of your mouth.

- ♥ Become aware of how much you say or others say during the day that is unnecessary.

   Begin to curb your desire to prattle. Put a brake on your tongue and resist the temptation to contribute to conversations that are going nowhere.

   Practice this in short segments and increase it gradually. It is a bit more challenging than it sounds.

- ♥ Using these **Four Golden Rules of Speech**, practice at work for just 15 minutes each day and gradually increase the time you do it. You may find this to be one of the hardest exercises you will encounter. With practice you will eventually catch yourself as the first words begin to be spoken and you realize that what you were going to say did not meet one of the criteria. It's OK to stop mid- word or sentence and just drop it. Always stop and think if what you are going to say is really beneficial and uplifting.

- ♥ Ask a friend to do this practice with you. Make it a fun experience and agree to continually call one another any time either of you catch the other stepping out of the boundaries of the **Four Golden Rules of Speech**. You will begin to see how incredible it is at how much of our time is spent in gossip and unnecessary verbal prattle. Take some time to be in the silent heart space with your friend. Practice silence. In silence some of the greatest exchanges of the heart can be made.

CHAPTER 22

Do You Love Your Heart?

Do you love your heart? In other words, do you love yourself? What are your feelings about your own self-worth? Now I'm not speaking of financial worth here, but genuine self-worth. Do you take care of yourself? Do you speak to yourself in kind and uplifting language during the day? Do you thank yourself for the courage it took to choose birth on this earth plane? Do you thank yourself every day for being a loving and caring individual or for being willing to try to change for the better? Do you forgive yourself if you feel you have done something wrong?

Self-worth is one of the biggest issues all of us face. We all need to love who we are no matter what body shape we decided to take or how unusual we may look. We need to learn to love ourselves no matter what our families may have felt towards us or how negative they were towards us, and we need to love ourselves no matter what degrading or cruel words an enemy may have said about us. Only from learning to love ourselves can we learn to love others. Take some time to think about the importance of this concept.

Can you think of someone who is never happy with themself? These type of people have a tendency to need and seek continual reassurance that they are OK, that they look alright, or that what they said was correct and so on. Their whole life is one of seeking this continual assurance they are fine. They have a tendency to repeat questions about their self-worth over and over again because of the need for someone else to validate them.

I would often see this when I worked in retail years ago. A customer would try on an outfit and then ask if I thought she looked good in it. You could tell she loved it but needed validation. I would always give my honest opinion, that's what I was there for, and if I felt it wasn't quite right I would give suggestions or ideas on how to enhance it or choose something else I felt would be more appropriate. For most people this was enough. They appreciated my opinion and went from there. But there were those who would ask me over and over and over again if I liked the outfit: Are you sure it looks right on me? What about my hips? Are you sure you like it? Now you wouldn't lie to me would you? Are you absolutely sure? Are you positive? Do you think my boyfriend will like it, or will he only see how big I am? Now I'm only going to ask you this one more time. Are you absolutely and positively sure this doesn't make my hips look too large? (And of course this was never the last question). All these questions are not about the outfit she is trying on, but about her own self-worth as a human being. What is interesting is that she didn't trust herself and seeks all her self-assurance and self-worth to be validated by someone else.

What about people who go around always putting others down or those that carry on an ongoing negative dialogue about anything and everything? We often think of people who put others down as having a huge ego and an "I'm better than you" syndrome, but what is truly going on here is that we mirror one another. If someone is always in the habit of being sarcastic towards others it is because they are not happy with themselves. In other words they don't love themselves (or have self-worth), so how can they love others, which consequently results in putting others down. When you love yourself you will love others and you will speak with great understanding and compassion towards everyone. It is that simple. What you say negatively about others reflects the exact state of how you feel about yourself. Begin to watch how others talk. It becomes fascinating to observe language from this standpoint once you are aware of how we are all mirrors for one another.

So how do you learn to love yourself, the very heart of your being? By approving of who you are. If you do not love yourself no one else is going to really love you either. How can they? It all starts with you. You are unique. You have so much to offer others in this world whether you clean toilets, raise children, or run a corporation. You are special. Start giving yourself good strokes and always speak to yourself in a loving, gentle, caring and understanding way; the same way as you would speak to a good friend or child. Become your own best friend. Teach yourself to go inside to validate who you are instead of seeking validation from outside. This will help you to develop your own self-worth. When you begin to see your own self-worth, you open a treasure chest of diamonds just waiting to shine your light on others. You become the one who helps others to see their own self-worth.

Inspiration Exercises

- ♥ Step 1: Take a few minutes and write down the parts of your being that you do not like and the negative comments you often make about yourself inwardly and outwardly. Keep a notebook of these observations.

- ♥ Step 2: Today be vigilant in listening to yourself talk to yourself about yourself. Are you giving yourself uplifting comments or are you putting yourself down? Just observe today what thoughts you are saying to yourself about yourself. Jot down notes this evening of the negative thoughts you were thinking during the day about your own being, like "I am so sick and will never recover," "I am so fat and ugly," "She could never love someone like me," "I wish I had the muscles and buff body he has," "No one likes me because I am so stupid." This evening sit down and write the opposite thought patterns such as the examples below.

I am making decisions that support my health right **now**.

I am deeply appreciative of my health and vitality right **now**.

My body vibrates with health and vitality right **now**.

I love and accept my body and who I am right **now**.

My thoughts, words, and actions support my health and well being right **now**.

I am intelligent and make good decisions right **now**.

I am worthy of good friends right **now**.

I am worthy of a beautiful girlfriend right **now**.

I make friends easily right **now**.

Make a whole page of affirmations for each challenge you feel you are dealing with. Then get into the feeling of what it would be like to be well, or how it feels to have that special girlfriend by your side. Affirm <u>and</u> feel. Every day take time to repeat outloud your affirmations and get into the feeling of having them already manifested. Repeat and feel first thing in the morning, outloud. Do the same on your work breaks. Go off by yourself or to your car if necessary to repeat them out loud. If that is not possible find a quiet place and repeat them silently to yourself. Then do them out loud before you go to bed. You are planting seeds in your subconscious. Let them grow and flourish. Do them day in and day out. You will begin to shift your awareness and your self-talk and become empowered to be the dynamic being you are meant to be. Begin to see your life change right before your very eyes.

- ♥ What about compliments? What do you say when someone gives you a compliment about something you are wearing? How many times have you said, "Oh this old thing?" or "Thanks, I've had this for years." I'm sure you can come up with many others. These comments have to do with self-worth also. You are putting yourself down. No one cares how old your outfit may be. Can you take a compliment gracefully and just say "Thank you?" When you receive a compliment, acknowledge this sweet gesture with a thank you, and that is all that's needed. Practice this trait and begin to honor and respect yourself and what you have.

- ♥ Write yourself a letter today imagining this is a letter from God thanking you for taking birth on this planet to help in its upliftment, for all you do for others and for how you take care yourself. What would God say to you? How would the letter be written? Let it come from the standpoint of infinite love and understanding, giving praise to you, what you stand for, and the wise being that you are. When you are finished, read it outloud to yourself. Keep it close at hand or put it in a sacred space and refer to it often.

CHAPTER 23

Do You Think With Your Heart?

Most people think that we think with our mind. Well we do, but have you ever thought about dropping into your heart first before the message goes through the mind and out the mouth? Sounds like it may take too long? In reality we can't afford not to do this.

What are your thoughts like? Are they positive or negative? You do have a choice, you know. The following is an exercise to show you just how you can change your negative upsetting thoughts in an instant. I love to do this whenever someone is grumbling or spewing out some negative rerun. I say to them. "Close your eyes for a few seconds; I want you to experience something. (This usually startles them but they do it). Now, think of some place or someone you absolutely love. (They will always get a smile on their face). Now, for the next five seconds feel what it's like to be in this special place or with this special someone. (Besides feeling it inside they usually begin to describe how wonderful it is)." Then I explain to them how easy it is to transport themselves to a positive place and how good it feels. They begin to get the picture. Do not dwell on the negative. You have a choice in what you think. This usually cures someone from complaining around me.

The negative and worry thoughts waste your energy, shorten your life, and draw into your life the negativities you dwell on. This is an age-old truth that has been proven time and time again. In fact there is a book titled *Your Body Believes Every Word You Say* by Barbara Hoberman Levine. She explains how your thoughts and words and the many nifty little colloquialisms that you use daily actually cause negative events and health issues in your life. For example, using the continual colloquialism, "That person is such a pain in the neck," can actually cause you serious neck problems. Once again, these are proven facts, dear ones. It is a book that I feel should be used as a primer from grade school on up. Start using positive thoughts and uplifting words now.

It always behooves us to stop and think about the kind of energy we are sending out even in our slightest actions of playfully making fun of something or someone. Here's an example of a whole group of people who didn't think. They are sitting together, laughing and telling stories. One of them jokingly says, "Everyone here except Jeff is intelligent enough to understand the punch line." Now everyone laughs, including Jeff, who knows that he is intelligent but doesn't always get jokes right away, but so what. Jeff doesn't really feel insulted. It's just the way the group talks and everyone is the butt of everyone else's jokes. It's over, forgotten, and the group is on to laughing about something else.

We really need to think about this incident though, because what really happened was that these words were cruel no matter how lovingly or jokingly they were delivered. What we think of as lightly teasing another or using sarcastic remarks and actions in our dealings with others hits the universe with such an incredible force you cannot imagine.

Every word you say is recorded in the skeins of time and comes back to the one who says them. The vibration from those words also hit the subtle bodies of everyone in that group. The words spoken in jest to Jeff are exactly what his subconscious mind recorded regardless of whether no harm was intended. Jeff heard, "Everyone here except me is intelligent enough to understand the joke." To the subconscious mind it doesn't matter with what intensity they were delivered, they are simply recorded in his mind and in his thought patterns (and you know what that can do over time - create a lot of self-worth issues). Along with that the person who said it was dishonoring another human being. Everyone lost in that conversation, even those who did not speak up on Jeff's behalf because they allowed and supported negative sarcasm to be directed toward another human being.

Do you begin to see the importance of the words we use even in the lightest of situations? What appears to be harmless even in jesting actually can and does cause great harm over time and we are doing ourselves a great disservice. Any time we put another person or anything down, even in jest, we have actually put ourselves down. We are but reflections and mirrors of one another. What we say to another we actually say to ourselves.

The words we use affect us on the deepest levels of our being whether they were meant to or not. When we truly learn to drop into the heart, we think about our words and actions and how they will affect others. Since the mind frequents places it becomes familiar with, let it frequent the space of the heart where loving and uplifting thoughts dwell; and from there let your thoughts come forth as kind and loving speech and actions.

Inspiration Exercises

- There are times in everyone's life when we find ourselves complaining. To break these patterns try the exercise in the second paragraph of this chapter. It works great when something is really nagging at you. All you have to do to replace your thoughts with something pleasurable. As you think, so it is. Voila! It is done. It works! Fill your life with positive thoughts. Keep replacing a negative rerun scenario with a thought that brings you joy.

- Put yourself in an observation mode today and listen to your co-workers, friends, acquaintances or whomever you banter back and forth with in so-called playful teasing. Remember teasing is just a thread away from sarcasm. Teasing very easily goes to slamming an individual or situation. It can be so subtle yet so hurtful. Calling each other rude names even in jest is not coming from a standpoint of love, honor, and respect for one another. Begin to look at the effect it truly has on another human being and start watching what you say to others in your playful banter. What you call another is what you are calling yourself.

- Practice with a friend and agree to remind one another any time either one of you say something that is derogatory in any way about another individual. Keep in mind that what you say to or about another is something you dislike or are saying about yourself. We are all mirrors of one another. Also keep in mind that when you hear someone give you a compliment of some kind, it is they who are complimenting themselves because once again that person is a reflection of what they see in you. Often times when someone gives me a compliment I acknowledge this fact and say, "Thank you, and the love you feel from me is but a reflection of the love that is in you."

CHAPTER 24

Do You Act From Your Heart?

How do you know when you are coming from your heart and not your mind? Just think of someone you love and you immediately drop into your heart. Then from that space let your actions and words come forth. To live from the heart means that every action, thought and word comes from the same space; the heart space. If you do this work upon yourself, it will soon become very natural for you to always be uplifting in everything you do.

Let's look at the action of speech. What happens is that most people don't drop into the heart before they open their mouth. Big trouble! Whenever any little irritation comes up they either have a ready abusive dialogue just waiting in the wings to blast another person or they just start rattling off the top of their head without thought of the consequences of their speech or actions upon another. That's acting from the mind.

It is one thing to say who you are on the surface but how you live your life is often something else altogether. You can tell the whole world how great you are but your actions tell the true you. Your walk and talk on this earth must be the same. We are coming to a point in consciousness where people are becoming so aware that it becomes very evident when one is saying one thing and doing another. Integrity is so important.

Several years ago I was with someone who had wanted to spend some time with me. It was a new acquaintance and I had attended a function where he had given a talk. I remember wincing at several of his comments in the way he described the type of work he did. His type of work was spiritual and lofty but throughout the conversation he was very sarcastic and disparaging. On one hand this person appeared to be very spiritual, but in his talking he displayed something different. It was not the most comfortable experience for me and there was definitely a missing element. His convictions didn't match his words. In other words his walk and talk weren't quite the same.

I later spent some time with this individual because I was curious as to what made him tick. He presented himself with the awareness of being in touch with his heart. There were many elements about him that showed he could be kind, caring, and spiritual but, of course, as we just mentioned, actions speak louder than words. As we were driving to our destination I began to observe language he would come up with when dealing with several challenging traffic situations, along with an on-going derogative dialogue he used in pointing out specific places along the way. One could look at the comments as being comical in a light sarcastic way, but to me it felt very disrespectful. His actions of speech were betraying who he felt he was and how he truly felt about himself. I could feel anger, resentment and irritation within him. His actions of speech were showing a great disrespect for himself and others. In other words he wasn't truly living or acting from the space of his heart. The heart will always come from a place of respect and honor for everyone and everything.

You are given situations every day in which the universe is training you on the spot. How will you react in any given situation? Positive and uplifting or negative and degrading? Your daily life is a laboratory for spiritual growth. You do not come on stage as one thing and when you go behind the curtain become something else. Your whole life is the stage. You need to remain the same no matter where you are, always being steady and giving your very best to the world in every circumstance. Hold the highest awareness of yourself and others. Act out of integrity with every experience put before you. Drop into your heart before you act or ever utter a word. Let your goodness shine forth and you will begin to experience divinity within everyone and everything.

Inspiration Exercises

- ♥ The action of speech: So many times we say something to a person only to immediately say something else in our mind as that individual walks away. As you interact with others this week notice any incongruities in your speech and mind patterns. For example, have you ever expressed to someone your encouragement about applying for a job stating that you know they will do well in the interview, while behind their back thinking they won't stand a chance of getting that position? Or maybe someone has expressed her excitement to you regarding a class they want to take and you are enthusiastic with her but thinking the whole time, "I've watched this scenario before and she will get bored within the first 5 minutes and drop out as usual." Begin to practice changing your thoughts. If your action of speech is positive on the outside, make sure you are sending blessings from your mind also.

- ♥ Take this week and observe others in their speech patterns where they profess to be something they are not. Perhaps it is someone who feels they are a good citizen yet never votes, or you see them littering. Watch your own actions also and start thinking how you can better match what you profess you are to the true colors you actually show the world. Put these incongruities to rest and begin to walk your talk. Let your actions always be the highest for yourself and all others.

- ♥ Look at your own life and the incongruities you show the world. Do your actions in the world correspond to your actions at home behind closed doors? Do you present to the world that you are clean, neat and fashionable, yet at home your beautiful clothes are strewn hither and yon and you haven't hung up a stitch of clothing for two weeks? Do you present yourself to the world as an upstanding husband at work and go home and abuse your wife? You are really not fooling anyone here except yourself. The universe knows what is going on. Let your actions on the outside portray your private life also. Begin to live in honor and respect in all areas of you life.

CHAPTER 25

Do You Work From Your Heart?

Every human being on this planet works in one form or another. Work simply means to perform actions in order to do or make something. We can work physically or work mentally, but we all work. This chapter is about doing all the things we do during the day with love, whether we consider them work or not. Whether we have an eight to five job or are in Hawaii on a vacation we are always performing actions. It's how we go about performing these actions that count in life.

The great saints of this world have told us over and again that it is not about getting the work done but in completing it with love. If we take every single task we do and perform it deliberately as if it is the most important task in our life right this instant, we would lead much happier lives. From a housewife washing the dishes to an architect designing a new home, from taking the kids to the park to play, to sitting at your desk inputting computer data, do everything deliberately and with love.

In today's chaotic world of "Let's see how much I can cram into today," step back and change your perspective. Ask yourself, "How can I get my work today accomplished with love?" What does it mean to do work with love? It means to be present in each moment and to do what is in front of you with your full attention. What usually happens is that we try to do three things at once. I knew a person who was always bragging about how she could do so many things all at the same time. I happened to visit her one day and observed her in action. Yes, she could do several things at the same time, but she wasn't really paying attention to any of them. They were rote activities and there was no pleasure in any of them for her. They were just tasks. And I'll have to admit I didn't really feel that she cared if I was there visiting or not. I was just one more task in front of her. To her it was sort of like a challenge. It's like watching TV, talking on the phone, fixing dinner, and deciding what you will wear to work tomorrow all at the same time. Sound familiar? I hope not. But if so, how rewarding is your life? Is the purpose of life to just rush through it and not enjoy it? I don't think so.

I have to admit there have been many times that I too have rushed through life and at certain times I still struggle with this because I am an achiever, a goer, and a doer. I have to remind myself once in a while to put the brakes on and remember to do just one thing at a time. When I do this I like myself so much more. By putting love into the simplest of actions I always do a better job than if I had rushed. The crazy thing is that it doesn't take me any more time to do it consciously, deliberately, and with love than if I had rushed.

How many of you have lived this scenario? This is an example of myself several years ago. I get up to get dressed and realize I need to wear my blue jeans for a function that day. I go through my closet to realize they are in the dirty clothes bin. I rush downstairs to put them in the washer to see that one of the kids did a load of wash and didn't put it in the dryer. I open the dryer to put the wet clothes in and realize that it's full of dry clothes.

As I'm bent over the clothes dryer I smell the cat box. I look over and sure enough it didn't get scooped out yesterday. I put the dry clothes on top of the dryer and clean the cat box to realize that we are out of cat sand, so I go upstairs to write it on a grocery list before I forget (cat sand is as essential as toilet paper). Now here I am upstairs again without having done anything about my blue jeans. Nothing was done with love, but in a total rush along with frustration, and I'm now standing there still in my pajamas trying to figure out what in the world brought me in here to write a grocery list when I'm not even dressed yet. I then go, "Oh yeah, I needed to wear my blue jeans today!" Back to square one. You could say that this is definitely due to a lack of planning; but for those of you working moms with husband, kids, and pets, you know better. There are several ways I could rerun this scenario and not have been so frustrated.

Over the years as I've taken the practice of completing my work with love, I find my state of mind becomes so peaceful. When I iron, I iron. When I wash the floor, I wash the floor. I'm not thinking about how fast I need to get it done and what I will do next. Remember that old saying, "Take time to smell the roses?" Well, that is all about doing things with love. The 'In-Basket' at work will always be there and it will always be full. That is its purpose in life. I have gone for weeks without seeing the bottom of my 'In-Basket' and I'm here to tell you it is OK. It's not the end of the world. If you die tomorrow someone would do your 'In-Basket'; I promise you. Why walk out of the office at the end of the day feeling frazzled and feel as if you didn't really accomplish anything, having that defeatist attitude that there is more work than you will ever be able to get done? Always just do what you can whether at work or at home. If it doesn't get done, it just doesn't get done. If you died in your sleep tonight, would you want to be remembered as the one who was able to keep her 'In-Basket' empty, or the one who took the time to be there for all who came to her no matter how busy she was?

Here's another way to look at trying to do things in a hurry. We have all been witness to this phenomenon. We're driving along at the speed limit going to our destination and someone comes rushing along weaving in and out of traffic, barely missing or sideswiping cars. This person is obviously in a rush. Pretty soon he is way up there and out of your sight. Then the next thing you know, two stoplights down the road there he is stopped at the same traffic light you are. All that rushing, stress, and dangerous driving was in vain. You just have to laugh, don't you? It has been proven time and again that driving fast and trying to get to your destination in a hurry is not effective. It's the same way with every task you complete. If you just slow down and do your actions with love, you will have a sweet sense of accomplishment and be at peace with yourself and the world.

Take time to breathe, and take time to plan your day so you're not rushing. The five minutes you spend in planning the day's activities will give you an order for the day and a sense of accomplishment even if you are only able to cross off one item. Also, do not overload yourself on your 'To Do' list. This will help you to be able to enjoy each task for just what it is. If you can't get everything done on your list then transfer it to tomorrow. Put love in every action because if you don't no one else will. The older you get the more you realize that nothing is more important than to live in the joy of the moment because this may be the only moment you have.

Inspiration Exercises

❤ Look at all the tasks you perform today from a new awareness and practice being in the moment. Are you really there for your children as you are playing blocks with them - are you really loving this time frame that you have with them and enjoying their laughter and this special time to be with them, or are you mentally trying to decide what to have for dinner tonight and if you will have to go to the grocery store first? Take each task and ask yourself, "Am I here right now, fully present and accounted for? Am I focused on my children in front of me and having a good time with them? Am I living in love for this very moment?" Every time your mind sets off in another direction bring it back to the task at hand and really get into it. Get into their joy and laugh with them. Continually practice this "in the moment awareness." Then observe how you feel at the end of the day having lived in those precious moments. You will begin to feel really good about yourself and life.

❤ You can do this exercise with absolutely any task or any person. Some of you will decide you want to try this but choose to do it on a day when you do not have much planned so it will be easier. I understand and this is fine. Keep practicing and then take it to a busier day and a busier one until all your days on this earth are filled with doing each individual task with great love and in the present moment, the only one you have.

❤ 'To Do' Lists: Those of you who make them and use them will tell everyone how important they are and how they do not know how they ever lived without doing this practice once they got into the habit. Sit down in the evening when it is quiet and write out the next day's goals or do it first thing in the morning. Have two, three, or four columns and title them. An example could be columns such as: <u>To Do</u> - list all the projects or items you want to do at home or at work or both, <u>To Go</u> - list all the places you need to run errands to that day, <u>To Call</u> - List all the phone calls you want to make, <u>To E-mail</u> - list the ones you know you want to send. On the backside of the paper you may even want to write columns for a more detailed description from the items you put on the front. An example might be put under the 'To Go' section such as the Drugstore - and list the items you need, <u>Grocery Store</u> - list items, etc. Be imaginative. You can get very detailed or keep it as simple as you want - just do it. It will help you organize your day to free the mind clutter of trying to remember or figure out how you will do everything. It will also allow you a better chance of being in the moment with each task that awaits you.

♥ Take just a moment and pause before you start each task today and breathe deeply for five breaths. Then also very consciously pause several times during each extended task and calmly and deeply breathe for five seconds or so to center yourself. Allow the breath of life to enter your lungs deeply and just 'be' in the present moment. This will not only help you feel centered but grounded as well.

CHAPTER 26

The Physical Heart?

Throughout this book we have been discussing the more esoteric aspects of being in the heart. Now I want to go to the other aspect and speak about the actual physical heart and taking care of it.

In a human, the physical heart reflects the total overall nutrition of your body. You are obviously aware that you need your heart to be able to survive, but did you know that every organ of the body would give its nutrition to the heart just to keep the heart pumping? In other words the body will sacrifice everything to keep the heart working. In autopsies done in concentration camps the two healthiest organs were the heart and brain. If there is no nutrition in the body to rob from, to give to the heart, your heart will stop functioning.

So what am I getting at here? I want to stress the importance of how nutrition affects the entire system and especially the heart. Not only is nutrition important for the heart but so is exercise and a balanced life style. Everything revolves around the hub of the heart. If you don't exercise and eat right you stand a good chance of gaining weight and having heart problems. If you do not lead a balanced life style there comes a point that you have stressed out for so long, you have heart attacks. It is important for you to have a healthy physical heart so you can offer the love and blessings we have been speaking of.

Isn't it interesting to note that even though this book is about the esoteric heart of love, the body itself will do everything possible to keep the physical heart alive? It is no wonder that we speak of coming from the heart, living in the heart, being in the heart, loving from the heart, as the place to be, even though it is not a physical space to which we are referring.

I'm not going to get into what you should and shouldn't do here as far as nourishing your body in both exercise and food. I just want to make you aware of the importance of both hearts in relationship to the divine. If you do not have a physical heart, in other words you've left this plane of existence, how can you help others? We are here to serve humankind with all our heart in whatever way our destiny is determined for us. We can make nutritional choices, exercise choices and the choice of a balanced and harmonious life style that either helps our heart or hurts our heart. The better care we give our physical heart and body, the better we feel, and the easier it is to offer the infinite treasures of our divine heart to the world.

Inspiration Exercises

♥ As with anything you do over time it becomes a routine, a regular practice. I encourage you to start doing something to exercise and energize your own being. Our bodies do like routine. It is one thing we can do for ourselves that does not necessarily have to change once we have it in place. Write out several ways in which you can exercise the body three to four times per week and then how you could achieve that with your daily schedule.

I personally am not an exercise buff, but many years ago I decided I had to start exercising for my own health so I started walking - for me the line of least resistance in exercising. Now I love to walk and hike. If it's winter and I have to be on a treadmill instead of outside I can be thinking how great this is for my sweet body and do uplifting affirmations and send blessings to individuals while on it. In the spring and summer I can walk in nature and be there in the moment watching and admiring nature and sending love and blessings to each and every leaf on every tree and to each blade of grass. Lately, after many years of thinking about this, I have taken up figure-skating and dancing lessons again. I am having a ball and I was amazed at the number of men and women from teens to those in their sixties and seventies getting exercise in my Salsa dance class. START TODAY to do something for the health of your physical heart.

♥ Take a walk through your local grocery store this week and look at the food that is available to you from the standpoint of the paragraph below. Then go to a healthy food store if there is one near you or make plans to visit one in a city near you. Start your own plan of how you can buy healthier foods. Always buy organic food when you can.

On our grocery store shelves in America today only approximately 5 percent of the food items that are available are good for us. The rest is literally dead food, canned, processed, full of pesticides, and of little or no nutritional value. Think about what you are feeding yourself and your children along with the long-term effects it will have on your entire being. The foods that are being consumed today result in poor health and disease-ridden bodies. The health of Americans is declining rapidly and disease is rampant. One of the main causes is a direct result of the foods we put in our bodies.

Become aware of the foods you eat, begin to eat organic foods and increase your support for organic growers. Only through the support to your body of proper nutrition will you be able to complete this life in health, for without it all other ambitions and good intentions are extremely difficult to practice and accomplish. We are put on this earth to be radiant beings, to grow emotionally, spiritually, and physically in health and to offer our help and service for the upliftment of others. We need to start with the food we put into our bodies.

♥ This evening jot down how you felt about your day. Was it a balanced day? Did you get time to rest during the day or play at all? Did you take time to nourish your soul through prayer or meditation? What about exercise? Did you rush from one thing to another? Where did your day go? Was it lived in contentment? Was it lived in harmony? Did you laugh and enjoy being in the present moment? Was it a day you would want to relive?

Now contemplate how you could have changed the day had you planned it better, or lived more in the moment, or transferred some items to tomorrow's agenda to lighten your load. It is so important that we balance our life styles to honor our existence in work, spirituality, play, exercise, and rest. I do not believe we were put on this planet to lead the incredibly complex, harried existence we see happening around us. What can you do to reach a more balanced style of living so you are honoring the divineness of your own existence? Be innovative and look at where you can change or rearrange your routines, work, chores, and everything that fills your life to a more balanced, higher way of being.

CHAPTER 27

The Walls of the Heart

How many of you have built walls around your heart to protect yourself? Sometimes it appears that if we open our hearts too much we become vulnerable, get hurt, walked on, and taken advantage of. As small children we are so open to the world and all it has to offer. As we get older, we are given situations and challenges which allow us to grow, and depending on our internal support channels, we take each challenge, process it mentally and then decide how we will then deal with the world from that day forward. We either allow a circumstance or challenge to enrich our lives or decide that this particular circumstance was so detrimental to us that we shut down and throw up these huge invisible fortresses around our heart to protect us from anyone or anything ever hurting us again. If we have decided to build a fortress then slowly, little by little, we decide this earth home is not such a great place to be and the walls get thicker. You know the rest of the story. We see angry, negative, vengeful people every day with walls around their hearts that are so thick you couldn't blow them away with dynamite.

As I stated before, depending on our support channels, environment, culture, family and friends, we either use the challenges of our life to grow stronger and become a wiser, more loving person, or we begin to shrink - not in physical size mind you, but in beginning to wrap ourselves tighter and tighter into ourselves to protect us from this world so that we can feel safe. I'm sure you have all seen people who have put so many walls around their heart that they are almost palpable. No matter what you try you can't seem to get past their barriers of lack of trust, hurt, jealousy, greed, or unwillingness to be free and enjoy life. Always playing the victim, they are either guarded in their actions and speech or spewing anger and venom at anyone who will lend an ear, always looking over their shoulder for the next person who is going to try to sabotage them.

If you are one of these people with what I call the "walled-heart syndrome" learn to begin to live in an open and loving, vulnerable position at all times. If you don't, your life will be anything but fun and joyous. Your life will continue on, as will the challenges you came in to learn from, whether you want them to or not, so it makes so much more sense to drop the beliefs that the world is out to hurt you. You came in to this life with a bank of predestined life circumstances that will unfold through you and for you throughout your life. These life experiences are here for you to learn to grow beyond your current boundaries and limitations into something wonderful and beautiful. How many times have you heard or read of people with really unfortunate circumstance after circumstance in their life, yet they are the most loving and caring people, with totally open hearts? They so often say about their experiences, "If it hadn't have been for thus and so experience I could not have learned to give of myself so deeply", "I never would have learned to have confidence in myself", or "I never would have learned to go beyond my physical disability."

In my early twenties I had a job where I worked with people who had catastrophic losses in their lives. Now I grew up as an only child, and pretty much had everything I needed or wanted, so my compassion wasn't so developed for those less fortunate than I.

The Walls of the Heart

When I first started working with these people I began to put up wall after wall of protection around my heart so I wouldn't have to get involved on an emotional level in dealing with their problems. It was too much for my heart to deal with. I was hearing them but not listening to them. I began to feel I wasn't relating to them the way I wanted to so I began to contemplate why. Once I could see what my pattern was and why I did this I very quickly began to shift my perception and began to break down these walls I had put up. I really began to listen intently to these precious, unfortunate people, and I would let my heart just melt. I began to feel great compassion towards every single person that sat across from me as they relayed their story. The interesting thing was that because I was now better able to connect with them through my heart, they too were better able to connect with me as I helped them to get their lives back on track. I grew stronger and they grew stronger. We both benefited by my openheartedness.

Your life was made for loving one another and every situation in the highest way possible so you can learn and grow. Every situation, whether you realize it or not, is there for your best interest, so let even the slightest walls around your heart crumble and give of yourself openly and lovingly to life. Offer your highest and best to each person and circumstance. You will begin to live an enchanted life that is filled with wonder when you allow the walls that surround your heart to dissolve.

Inspiration Exercises

- ♥ Think about an instance in your life where you may have completely closed down and the effect it had on how you began to view your life from that point on. Try to think of one that may have happened several years ago. Write down and examine the feelings you had during what you felt was an unfortunate incident or relationship. What did you do to compensate for the challenge? Did you grow from it? Did you look at it as a learning experience to see what you might have done differently, or how you could have reacted differently? How did it affect your life then? How does it affect your life now? Do you have walls around your heart to protect you from anything like that ever happening again?

  What would it look like if you could let the barriers you have set up dissipate? Now look at the situation and try to see the lesson behind it. Gently begin to allow yourself to step out of fear and negativity and begin to embrace the experience for what it was, perhaps an experience to help you grow and develop in compassion, an opportunity to love another through incredible odds, or whatever fits here for you. Start being more open and vulnerable to life again.

- ♥ Think of the opposite situation too, where you let yourself be vulnerable and loving even when you felt you could get hurt again. Write down how that felt. What was it like to let feelings run through you, be an observer of them, and be affected by them in a compassionate way, learning the lesson it was trying to teach you and then moving on, keeping your heart open and loving for the next experience? If you can understand the lesson behind the challenge, very often you will never have to go through that particular experience again because it has been learned.

You will keep repeating patterns until you learn the lessons you came here to learn. This is how this planet is set up. And if you do go through a similar experience again with an open heart you will know how you were able to cope with it before and you came out of it just fine. Perhaps the lesson this time around is similar in its aspects but there may be an entirely new lesson to learn from it. A good example of repeating the same lesson is when you may divorce someone for some reason but let's say it is because your spouse was abusive to you. Then you turn around and end up marrying another individual who treats you the same way. This is because the lessons have not been learned from the first marriage, the lesson here being one of self-worth, to know that you are a worthy and divine individual and deserve to be treated with love, honor and respect. Until the lesson is learned, husbands three, four, etc. will more than likely be the same.

Practice letting walls of protection dissolve and dissipate. Offer your fears to God and keep your heart open and loving. Move out of fear, anger, and hatred. Step into being the open, sweet, and vulnerable soul that lives by the principle of love from the heart.

Just BE from the Heart

All it takes is one small act of love, followed by another small act of love, followed by another small act of love, and before you realize what has happened you begin to see you are living in that divine heart space, the space of love itself. Don't let anything get in your way of love. Every moment of life is so precious. How many times have I heard someone say, "I just can't wait until my shift is over...", or, "I wish this day would end, nothing has gone right today." Just stop for a minute and look at what you said about precious time. Never, never wish away time, but live deliberately in each moment knowing this is all you have. Walk deliberately upon this earth sending blessings and love to all. Let your energy flow through each footstep, through the earth, clear across to the other side, knowing that people across the world are receiving your blessings. Yes, you do have the power to do that.

May you all be filled with light, and may sunshine and God's love surround you always.

With much love,
Julie

About the Author

Julie Anderson lives in La Jolla, California where she has dedicated her life to the upliftment of humanity through her clear and powerful vision to bring healing, science, and spirit together to help individuals become whole and holy. From the tender age of twelve she had a deep longing to know God and felt intuitively that one day she would be able to go beyond the paradigms that exist today, not only to help others get well, but to teach the importance of the connection to spirit and how it plays one of the key roles in health.

She graduated from WSU with a BA in Education. Her yearning for healing was brought about through a childhood illness treated by Edgar Cayce. This drew her to study many myriad forms of alternative health practices. In her quest for spiritual knowledge, Julie was drawn to India where she studied under one of the world's greatest living masters where she lived in monasteries for five years.

Julie's confidence, enthusiasm, humility, and spirituality bring forth this new paradigm for integrated health and allow her to empower and assist others in regaining a healthful and heart-centered life thus helping to dissolve the veil that divides humans from higher levels of consciousness.

In addition to spiritual coaching and writing, Julie also does commercial property management. She has two grown children and enjoys most doing spiritual practices and exploring the Pacific beaches

Contact Information for Julie Anderson

Julie Anderson
c/o ICAN Publishing Company
7520 Charmant Drive
Suite 1014
San Diego, CA 92122

For information or personal consultations,
e-mail Julie at: **julie@destinationheart.com**

Please send Julie your experiences of stepping into the virtues of heart-based living, which either resulted from your reading of this book or from personal experiences you would like to share. Your suggestions and feedback are welcomed.

Website: www.destinationheart.com

Index

Notes and stories by chapter:

Chapter 1	Welcome
	Fast food chain
Chapter 2	Courage
	Divorce and superwoman
	Pizza parlor incident
Chapter 3	Faith
	Lost in Bombay
Chapter 4	Listen
	Listening feedback skills
	Calm irate people down
Chapter 5	Beauty
	Auswich concentration camp
Chapter 6	Compassion
	I'm sorry/sympathy/compassion
	Long time negative unhappy person
Chapter 7	Humility
	Organization that picks one person for courageous act
Chapter 8	Wisdom
	Snowboard incident
Chapter 9	Patience
	Rushing through chores
	Car/always bring something to do
Chapter 10	Gentleness
	Leadership from the highest/your boss
	Nordstrom/moving up corporate ladder too fast
Chapter 11	Gratitude
	Bombay/girl on three legs
	Hawaiian Island hurricane

Chapter 12	Enthusiasm
	Indian greeting card
Chapter 13	Blessings
	Jilted by boyfriend
	TV/newspaper blessings
	Bless everyone and everything all the time
Chapter 14	Take Care of Others
	Car accident/out of body experience
Chapter 15	Forgive Others
	Parents can't give you what they don't have
	Families greatest place to practice – push buttons
	Feedback skills
Chapter 16	Love the Animals
	Bird story
	Deer story
Chapter 17	Heart Smiles
	Various types of smiles
	Department store training
	Train ride in India
Chapter 18	Follow Your Heart
	Ferryboat ride
	My story/wanting to know God
	Old-age writers group
Chapter 19	Meditation
	Instructions
Chapter 20	Living
	Your offerings to the world
	Each minute is new
Chapter 21	Speech
	4 Gates of speech

Chapter 22	Loving
	Our need to love ourselves/self-worth
	Retail customer/"Are you sure I look good?"
	Positive affirmations
Chapter 23	Thinking
	Complaining/close your eyes for a minute
	Understanding the joke incident
	Teasing/sarcasm
Chapter 24	Acting
	Walking your talk/astrologist story
Chapter 25	Working
	Getting work done with love
	Multitasking
	Blue jeans day story
	Cars speeding incident
Chapter 26	Physical Heart
	Nourishment
	Exercises
	Balanced and harmonious life style
Chapter 27	Walls of the Heart
	Walled-heart syndrome
	Building walls around my job story

The Heart
The Final Destination

Measure your life in love.
—Julie Anderson

Quick Order Form

Fax orders: 858-658-0446. Send this form.

Telephone orders: Call toll free: 866-525-6134
Have your credit card ready.

Email orders: orders@destinationheart.com

Postal orders: ICAN Publishing Co., Julie Anderson,
7520 Charmant Dr. Ste. 1014, San Diego, CA 92122-5031

Please send the following books. I understand that I may return them for a full refund.

_____
_____
_____

Please send more FREE information on:
❑ Other books   ❑ Speaking/Seminars   ❑ Consulting

Name: _____
Address: _____
City: _____ **State:** _____ **Zip:** _____
Telephone: _____
Email address: _____

Sales tax: Please add 7.75% for products shipped to California addresses.

Shipping by air
U.S.: $4.05 for first book and $2.00 for each additional product.
International: $9.50 for first book; $5.00 for each additional product (estimate).

Payment: ❑ Cheque   ❑ Credit card:
       ❑ Visa   ❑ MasterCard   ❑ AMEX   ❑ Discover

Card Number: _____
Name on card: _____ Exp. date: _____

Thank you for your order.